Additional Praise for
10 Financial Mistakes You Should Avoid

"Are you worried about how to diagnose your financial health? Read this book. Stephen Ng helps you understand common financial ailments, offering a no-nonsense approach to planning for your financial future."

—VICKI RACKNER, MD
President, Medical Bridges

"This is a terrific guide on the ever-changing (and sometimes confusing) road to financial goals....readers can appreciate the financial road signs found in this easy-to-navigate financial guide."

—MARSHA FRIEDMAN, CEO, EMSI
Publication Relations Corp.

"I've known Stephen for a number of years, having worked with him and his clients. This book is an insightful guide to navigating your financial future."

—YALE S. HAUPTMAN, ESQ
Elder Law Attorney

"The Bible says: God's blessing makes life rich; nothing we do can improve on God. (Proverbs 10:22, The Message). If you're looking for practical ways to help manage your wealth, this is a must-read book. I plan to buy copies to share with my friends and family."

—REVEREND HOWARD LI
Senior Pastor, Trust In God Baptist Church

About the Author

Stephen is a Chartered Life Underwriter, a Chartered Financial Consultant, and a Certified Estate Planner. As the founder and manager of the Essex & Union County, New Jersey business-networking group, Stephen leads a team of more than 1,700 business professionals, helping them grow as individuals and make positive contributions to the community; he has assisted over 300 families and currently oversees over 100 million dollars of his client's assets. In 2011, Stephen was listed in the Champions Circle & the Million Dollar Club with SagePoint Financial, Inc. In 2010, he was in the top twenty-five producers and listed in the Champions Circle with SagePoint Financial, Inc. In 2005 and 2008, Stephen was named the Top Producer with American General Securities, Inc.

Stephen is married and has three children. He serves as a deacon at Trust In God Baptist Church in New York City.

10

FINANCIAL MISTAKES

YOU SHOULD AVOID

Strategies Designed to Help Keep
Your Money Safe and Growing

STEPHEN S. K. NG

CLU, CHFC, CEP

Hardcover: 978-0-692-46360-4
Paperback: 978-0-692-46361-1
eBook: 978-0-692-46362-8

Library of Congress Control Number: 2015904199

Stephen S.K. Ng. Registered Representative
Investment Advisor Representative

Securities and Investment Advisory Services offered through SagePoint Financial, Inc., member FINRA/SIPC.

Insurance services offered through Stephen Ng Financial Group LLC, are not affiliated with SagePoint Financial Inc.

To my wife, Elizabeth,
and my children, Lois, Loanne, and Jaron:
You are my inspiration and motivation.

C O N T E N T S

ix
ACKNOWLEDGMENTS

1
INTRODUCTION

17
STRATEGY #1
Have a Plan!

25
STRATEGY #2
Understand Time Horizons

37
STRATEGY #3
Preserve Your Investments

45
STRATEGY #4
Understand Taxation

Contents

55

STRATEGY #5
Educate Yourself

65

STRATEGY #6
Diversify

75

STRATEGY #7
Seek Advice

83

STRATEGY #8
Risk Management Strategies

95

STRATEGY #9
Understand Longevity Risk

105

STRATEGY #10
Understand the Sequence-of-Return Risk

115

EPILOGUE
The Three Stars

ACKNOWLEDGMENTS

Thank you to all my clients over my twenty-two years of practice. As your financial advisor, you have allowed me to help you and your families to grow and preserve your wealth.

To all my many coaches, team members, and pastors: Your love and advice have allowed me to stay humble and to improve myself each day so that I can help others in my practice.

Finally, to God be the glory. He is the ultimate giver of wisdom. He refreshes me each day so that I can refresh others and be a blessing to them.

Introduction

It's amazing when you think about how well-educated most Americans are when it comes to their professions and careers, and how uneducated so many people are with regard to their finances.

American society is awash in information about money. We are constantly bombarded with news stories about the business world, stock market reports, investment opportunities, predictions, and hot tips. But most people still end up making decisions based on emotion and lack of accurate, complete information.

This wouldn't matter so much if our retirements weren't on the line.

Most people don't even want to think about retirement. They see it as a far-off time when they will somehow have magically accumulated all the money they need to jet around the world, pay for their grandchildren's education, or otherwise hang out and have fun.

If you're like most people, the last time you believed that someone would magically put money under your pillow while you slept was when the tooth fairy came calling! But now we're adults, and more and more adults are unprepared for the reality of their retirement years. They are unprepared because, sad to say, they tend to make the same set of mistakes that so many millions of others around them are making. The purpose of this book is to show you how *not* to make those mistakes, so that when you choose to retire, you are better prepared.

Let's consider the recession of the early 2000s. Say you worked for one of the major technology companies, and prior to the technology meltdown in 2001, your 401(k) plan had a value of $2.4 million and held a large amount of your technology employer's stock. Less than a year later, as technology stocks plummeted, so did the value of your 401(k)—all the way down to $240,000. You would have lost 90 percent of this nest egg.

Most people we meet don't have $2.4 million in the bank! They often have far less. But they are still subject to making the same mistakes that so many of their friends and neighbors are quietly making, all but ensuring that either they will not be able to retire, they will have to work at least part time during their so-called retirement years, or they will outlive their money.

In the hypothetical case I just mentioned for illustrative purposes, overexposure to technology stocks, specifically the equity of one's company, destroyed virtually all hard-earned wealth.

It's my job to help make sure this doesn't happen to you. I've had the privilege of working as a financial advisor for the past twenty-two years. Over the course of that time, I have helped thousands of people recognize the key mistakes that they had been making, either through emotion or lack of information. I get tremendous joy helping clients and their families on a path toward a financially sound retirement. The purpose of this book is to share with you what I have learned working with all these individuals and couples over the past twenty-two years. I have identified ten key mistakes that people tend to make, and I'm going to show you not just why people make those mistakes and what they mean, but also, more importantly, how to try to avoid them.

In years past, people could count on the government or their employer to meet their financial needs in the relatively short window between retirement and death. Today, with the advances in medical technology, and a greater commitment to eating healthy and getting exercise, we're living so much longer. In fact, the average male lives to eighty-five, and the average female lives to the age of ninety! These are just averages—you could certainly be one of those fortunate people who lives on into their mid-nineties or even crosses the century mark. It sounds great … as long as you don't outlive your money!

The ten mistakes we'll discuss in this book are guidelines to prevent outliving your money, whether you pass away early, late, or "on time" from an actuarial standpoint. There's no reason for you to be working so hard your whole life only to fail to have the money that you could have had, if only you had avoided the sorts of things we will discuss in detail in this book.

Before I became a financial advisor offering guidance in all areas of my clients' financial lives, I started off selling insurance. That's when I discovered the first mistake that so many people make—they are underinsured. Maybe having a $100,000 life insurance policy gives you peace of mind, a sense that if something should happen to you, your loved ones will be taken care of. But there's a huge difference for me as the insurance agent delivering a check to the spouse of someone who has just passed away in the amount of $100,000 versus $1 million or $5 million. The reason I mention this is that even people who have taken some steps toward protecting themselves and their loved ones may simply have not done enough. I advised my clients that they should try to have six to ten times their annual earnings in life insurance. Anything less than that is not likely to cover the cost of a mortgage, children's education, and other life emergencies. The last thing any of my clients would desire is for their spouses to be in financial trouble if they were to pass away at an early age. So even people who are well-intentioned still make the mistake of not doing all that they need to do. Having the right amount and type of insurance is a critically important question that we'll talk about in this book.

I'm sure there are other things we would rather think about! So if you consider that we are talking about protection and care for your loved ones—which is a positive—instead of insurance, which is something no one likes to think about, that section of the book might be a little more palatable!

Another common mistake that investors make is trying to get too much too quickly. Another story from my early years in the industry: I saw many clients around the time of the tech bubble. I placed many of them in investments that bore moderate risk, and they were earning around 8 percent a year on their overall portfolios. But many of them weren't happy. "My nephew's making 80 percent!" one would exclaim. "I'm only making 8 percent!"

I tried to explain to each client that the high-flying tech stocks in which friends or family had invested were more likely to crash to earth than grow all the way to the sky, but some wouldn't listen. They got into tech stocks, the year 2000 came around, and you can guess the end of the story. When many of them came back to me a year or two later, their portfolios showed great losses. We need to understand that all investing involves risk, including the loss of principal—but we can take a thoughtful approach that seeks to help mitigate extreme loss and avoid certain financial pitfalls.

Mistakes can be very painful. Many people were spooked when the next market crisis came along in 2008. Did you have any trouble during the bubble? Not for those who stuck true to their long-term financial track and did not sell when the market was down. Those who led with their emotions instead of their intellect did sell at the bottom of the market, fearing that it would go down even further. But it's still America, and we're still open for business! I don't need to tell you that the stock market came roaring back after 2008, almost doubling in the seven years since the downturn. So we can see that emotion plays much too large a role in the thinking of many investors.

It's hard not to be emotional, though. After all, we're talking about money—one of the most emotional—and indeed volatile—subjects around! We are constantly bombarded with information, whether it's on CNN or one of the financial networks, or perhaps even the AARP. So often, I see investors make the mistake of taking a single, solitary piece of information—which may not even have been all that accurate to begin with—and then making a major portfolio decision based on that "factoid." Tell the truth—maybe you've done this yourself at some point! If you have, you're not alone. Millions of people act with their hearts instead of their heads when it comes to their money. Of course, this is a major mistake. The wiser course is to try to mitigate your risk, either by offloading it onto an insurance company, by using a fixed annuity—a process I'll explain later in the book—or by "staying in your shoes" and not chasing returns that are likely unsustainable in this or any other market.

The people I work with most frequently are in what the Prudential Insurance Company calls the "retirement red zone." They are between the ages of fifty and sixty-five, and they are either starting to think about retirement or have actually begun their retirement years. If you're a football fan, you know that the term "red zone" refers to the last twenty yards on the field before the end zone. Mistakes made in the end zone are extraordinarily costly. That's true in football, and it's also true in the "retirement red zone." Investors simply cannot afford to make a major mistake at this point in their financial lives.

I work hard to explain financial concepts in such a way that people can grasp the essence of what I'm actually saying. Sometimes financial advisors seem to speak in a language all their own that the layperson cannot understand. Are they doing it on purpose? Do they want people to be confused? Hard to say. I try to explain to people, in clear terms, what I believe they need to do and why, so as to protect their money now and help it grow as time goes on.

Let me give some more examples of the kinds of situations people get themselves into, either because they don't know any better or because they let emotions—typically fear or greed—drive their actions. Let's talk about taxes. Let's take for example investors with high-paying jobs, making half a million dollars a year. That's a fantastic amount of money for someone to earn, but the problem is that from January to June, it's as if they're working for the IRS, not themselves.

This is true for just about all of us. The concept that most people don't know about relates to tax evasion versus tax avoidance. *Tax evasion* is illegal, and you can end up in stripes! This is the sort of thing people do when they try to move money to the Cayman Islands, the Bahamas, Switzerland, or other offshore "banking havens." But all you need to do is Google the names of some of the top Swiss banks to discover that the IRS is breaking down the walls of secrecy and privacy that have traditionally protected those offshore accounts. The IRS certainly does not take a very tolerant stance toward people who try to evade our tax laws. Financial and criminal penalties are commonplace today for such people.

On the other hand, there is a concept called *tax avoidance*. Tax avoidance, if practiced in accordance with the United States tax code, is perfectly legal. It means that you manage to hold onto more of your money by finding ways to keep it out of the hands of the U.S. Treasury. Judge Learned Hand, one of the most respected jurists of the twentieth century, put it this way in a leading court case later affirmed by the United States Supreme Court: "Anyone may arrange his affairs so that his taxes shall be as low as possible; he is not bound to choose that pattern which best pays the treasury. There is not even a patriotic duty to increase one's taxes. Over and over again the courts have said that there is nothing sinister in so arranging affairs as to keep taxes as low as possible. Everyone does it, rich and poor alike, and all do right, for nobody owes any public duty to pay more than the law demands."

I teach my clients that when it comes to taxation, there are three types of money—taxable, tax-deferred, and tax-free. Most hardworking people have a lot of the first two, but they don't have a lot of tax-free dollars. It is rewarding to discover ways to move money into a tax-free "bucket"—and that can often include the income they receive, as would be the case with the professional making half a million dollars a year I mentioned a moment ago. Simply put, it's a mistake to overpay your taxes, and it's a mistake not to know how to avoid taxes in a legal and ethical manner. We will address this topic later in this book.

Another common mistake that people make relates to their overall portfolios. Typically, individuals own a combination of stocks and bonds. In simplest terms, stocks are usually more volatile and bonds are traditionally more of a conservative investment. One of the most common terms that investors hear is *asset allocation.*[1] Whenever I mention asset allocation to my new clients, I can see their eyes starting to roll backwards with boredom! They think they know all that stuff already—small cap versus medium cap versus large cap; domestic versus international—that sort of thing. They think they've got the whole asset allocation business handled.

In fact, they're often making a mistake. In my experience, besides taking the steps in asset allocation, there is something that very few investors—or even advisors—discuss. It's called the Efficient Frontier Theory, and it is so highly regarded that its creators were awarded the Nobel Prize for coming up with it. The Efficient Frontier Theory makes a

---

1 *Asset Allocation* does not guarantee a profit or protect against a loss in a declining market. It is a method used to help manage investment risk.

convincing case that most investors misallocate their investments when it comes to stocks and bonds. They just get the mix entirely wrong! The Efficient Frontier Theory teaches that the best mix for stocks and bonds is often 50-50, which is very different from what most investors—including most aggressive investors—tend to do. When we focus on the Efficient Frontier Theory when it comes to an individual's portfolio, we're trying to create the highest return with the least risk. In other words, the key phrase is not asset allocation; it's *risk-adjusted return*. Failing to focus on risk-adjusted return, as you can imagine, can be a major mistake.

We spoke earlier in this introduction about longevity risk—meaning that the longer you stick around, the greater the possibility that you can outlive your money. This can be a terrible situation for many people. Even those who follow the traditional "rules" of investing are unwittingly putting themselves at risk. Whether you have $100,000 in your portfolio or a million dollars, if you are following the commonly offered guidance to take out no more than 5 percent a year, standard mathematics tells us that you'll likely be in trouble twenty short years from today. Numbers don't lie. And if the market happens to be going down at the time that you retire—what people in our industry call the *sequence of return risk*—you can actually run out of money even sooner than you would have had the market been going up when you retired. Failing to understand that risk is potentially an extremely expensive mistake.

I've organized this book in terms of the ten mistakes people make because I want to get your attention! The fact that you're reading this book shows me that you are motivated to overcome one of the biggest mistakes in our society—an educational system that doesn't teach finance at all. You can get a Ph.D. from Harvard in fifty different subjects and have learned no basics at all along the way about finance or the economy. Or perhaps in your younger years you were not motivated to learn about money. Either way, financial planning turns into crisis management. The good news is that wherever you are, no matter how close to retirement, there are always things we can do to improve your investing strategy and help you remedy the mistakes that you might possibly have made in prior years.

We all know the old adage, "Failing to plan means planning to fail." I'm going to give you a way of creating a plan for yourself that allows you to take baby steps and start on the right road toward a happy, financially healthy retirement. There's nothing wrong with reaching out for help and getting educated. You do need to know about investments, taxation, insurance, retirement, and estate planning, especially if you are in that "red zone"—the ten to fifteen years prior to retirement.

It's also important not to view those five components of financial planning—investments, taxation, insurance, retirement, and estate planning, once again—as discrete, unconnected items. Instead, I will show you how to take a "macro perspective" so that you can make correlations among these five components. You'll have a view of both the forest and the trees.

I also work with many young people, and if you're still in your twenties or thirties, this book is for you just as much as it is for older readers. Your concerns and time frame are different, of course, but young people are prone to the same mistakes I'll be talking about in this book as their older friends and family.

Like most people, you might spend more time planning your vacations than planning your retirement at the time you first pick up this book. Maybe you spend more time determining which new car to buy than determining which investment products would be most valuable to your portfolio. My hope is that six months from now, that balance will be shifted somewhat in favor of devoting time to financial planning.

I mentioned the phrase *time frame* a moment ago. Most people approaching retirement think that their time horizon for investing is relatively short. But the reality is that if you are fifty-five today, and you live to the ripe old average age of eighty-five, an investment you make today has thirty years to grow and blossom! So your time frame, even if you are older, is much greater than you think.

We will discuss strategies that are designed to help protect against significant losses in the market. We will also discuss steps you can take to help grow and preserve your wealth, and how to diversify[2] effectively and have a number of different eggs in your retirement basket. As J. Paul Getty said, "Money is like manure. You have to spread it around or it's going to smell!" There's nothing like the sweet smell of financial success, and that's the fragrance I want you to be enjoying for the rest of your life!

There are so many other concepts we could get into here, but by now I think you see what awaits. In this book I will share with you ten strategies for overcoming the ten biggest mistakes that people make. You may only be making two or three, but why should you limit your financial horizons? My desire is that you will take the necessary steps to plan for your financial freedom and success ... now and later.

Learning these ten strategies, I hope, will be a very exciting journey for you. I'm honored to take that journey with you. Together, we can create a path toward reaching your

---

2 Diversification does not guarantee a profit or protect against a loss in a declining market. It is a method used to help manage investment risk.

financial goals and be aware of common financial potholes. The effort that you make reading and applying the concepts in this book puts you ahead of all those who failed to plan or take their financial well-being seriously. So let's get started!

STRATEGY #1

Have a Plan!

It happens to us all at times—we're either disinclined or too busy to prioritize forward thinking. Perhaps we don't realize we should be thinking long-term, worrying about something beyond this week's bank balance. Or maybe we have a feeling we should be considering our retirements or savings, but we're overwhelmed by the enormity of those words, or fearful of our inability to decide among the multitude of options.

In any case, one thing is clear. We need a map to navigate our own financial futures, no different from the map we might use to set sail across the Atlantic Ocean to Europe. The map, the compass, the GPS ... all of these tools work in concert and contribute to a master plan that hopefully sees us to shore. Similarly, a set of tools and strategies are needed to direct the course of our financial futures.

As I mentioned earlier, a prudent financial plan is composed of five unique pieces, each equally important: investments, taxation, insurance, retirement, and estate planning. Education planning is a sixth component for those of you with children. These areas are all interrelated, one piece affecting the outcome of another decades later.

Any financial plan is personalized to your stage of life. It changes over time to reflect your marital, family, and professional status. A couple with young kids, for example, has a very different looking plan than a retired older couple. The young couple's plan must emphasize insurance planning and education planning, namely life insurance policies and savings for college in the form of 529 plans. And because a family needs a stable home, this life insurance policy must also generally be high enough to protect their mortgage.

Let's say you've recently married your college sweetheart. You've been working on a scrapbook of wedding ideas and house furnishings for years, and you know you should start putting the same effort into future planning for your joint finances. After your happy engagement, you come to me to formulate a strategy, putting all of the above into action. I know you'll feel more comfortable now that you're thinking ten steps ahead fiscally, saving up for college funds for kids to come. The peace of mind to be gained by starting early is a blessing to newlyweds.

Now, an older couple's financial plan raises a different set of questions. Such a plan stresses retirement planning, and is mainly concerned with the distribution of retirement income accumulated over the couple's lifetimes. If my clients are middle-aged, we review their taxes to make sure they are maximizing tax breaks and investing for a long life, courtesy of our century's medical advances.

No matter your age or marital status, these plans contain strategies for your present and future financial situation, plans that allow you to make confident fiscal decisions without second-guessing your choices. Imagine the chaos if a homebuilder began construction without the architect's blueprints for the finished home. Or if a football team entered a tense playoff game without any articulated strategy. In either situation, there would be no clear path forward.

Financial plans, like game plans in sports or architectural renderings, resolve this potential confusion. In the following pages, we'll talk about Strategy #1, having a plan—and why you need one. Considering the uncertainty of our global economy today, this information is more important than ever. If you want to learn how to better manage your finances and seek professional advice on areas such as investments, retirement planning, insurance, and taxes, you've come to the right place—keep reading.

What's a Financial Plan?

Let's start with the basics. You're probably wondering what a financial plan looks like, and how the process of formulating one works. It's fairly simple in the beginning. And the control it will bring you regarding your finances will surely make the small upfront investment of time a worthwhile one.

First, I interview my clients. When we meet, I want to know your goals and objectives. I want to understand your complete financial history and learn all of the necessary information to formulate a smart strategy. If you are coming with a spouse, I listen to and record both of your financial situations and goals. Sometimes a husband and wife might want to retire at different ages. Or perhaps they see themselves with different lifestyles in retirement. Now, I'm not a marriage counselor, but I do need to please both of my clients and make sure that a joint financial plan for a couple or a family reflects the interests, situations, and aims of all parties involved.

I then enter all the relevant information into a financial planning software program. The software produces a document of roughly ten to twenty pages, entirely personalized to you. It takes into account your current situation, and projects the range of possibilities going forward.

Each of the five (or six) components we discussed earlier is addressed in its own section. The recommendations are far from one-size-fits-all. If a couple comes to me seeking advice for educational planning, they'll need guidance on building up savings for a college fund. If they're figuring their young kids will attend a state school and not an expensive private university, their college fund and savings plan will accordingly look a certain way.

We'll calculate what they would need eighteen years in the future, taking into account inflation and the average growth of their portfolio. We'll juggle their monthly expenses to cover these savings so that they will be ready once their children reach college age.

Now, the education piece of the puzzle is simple enough to figure out. The next step is considering several segments of the plan together. Most of life is learning how to balance, and financial planning is no exception. When money is tight, clients will often say to me, "Shouldn't I prioritize school savings over retirement, since my kids will be in college long before I plan on retiring?" This urge to prioritize is natural, but it can be risky.

We can never predict whether things will continue going as expected. Let's say the primary breadwinner in a family were to pass away. In a sad situation such as this one, educational planning alone won't be enough. The earlier decision to forgo life insurance—a choice made because the monthly payments were deemed a lower priority than college savings—will likely have negative consequences.

This is a good example of why financial plans use a number of strategies and take into account various outcomes. Life is unpredictable, and I work to help you respond to any changes.

Who Benefits From Having a Financial Plan?

Sometimes prospective clients come to me wondering if they "qualify" for financial planning advice. My answer is, universally, of course! You don't need to earn a certain amount of money per year, or be a minimum age, or maintain a minimum amount of money in a bank account or invested in the stock market in order to have a financial plan. Anyone and everyone benefits from having a personalized roadmap to their financial future.

Having a financial plan is not only for very high earners, or those advanced in age. If you want to accumulate wealth and reach that next income bracket, a financial plan will guide you in the right direction. It does so by defining your goals and matching your spending, saving, and investing habits to these objectives. Moreover, it will bring to light any fiscal mistakes being made and changes that are necessary in order to reach the financial heights you hope for. Lastly, it can illustrate future risk and help you prepare for a number of situations you might be faced with years down the road. Just as a car requires tune-ups when making plenty of long road trips, sometimes a financial plan might need slight adjustments when your circumstances change. The plans I design with my clients are fluid, reflecting their lives and changes in the economy.

Preserving Your Wealth

My practice is dedicated to growing and preserving your wealth. The most common mistake I see is people trying to grow their money without any preservation strategies. If you're not educated in how to invest wisely, taking excessive risks with investments is an easy trap to fall into. We must always have a strategy to help manage the ups and downs of the market.

Sometimes, people are initially scared to face the facts. But I've found that almost all of my clients find their financial plans empowering. Having a thorough and honest outlook on the numbers makes the whole process less daunting. In some cases, people realize they do have that extra bit of cash to take a vacation with their family, or donate to a cause they've been wishing to support.

This is a happy realization, and it might be yours if we spend just two or three hours going over your financial information together. The process of making a plan is pretty short.

If you wake up in the morning with a desire to see the big picture on your finances, we can have that picture painted together by that afternoon. Hopefully, you'll be better able to focus on your goals, and you'll understand what it will take to reach them. You'll learn how to balance competing financial priorities. And you'll end the day feeling that your financial life is headed in the right direction.

STRATEGY #2

Understand Time Horizons

Once you decide to have a financial plan, you need to consider the time horizons of various portions of that plan. When it comes to planning for retirement or choosing between investment strategies, understanding time horizons is crucial to deciding which path matches your predicted financial needs.

Clients often ask me, "How much of my portfolio should be in the stock market or in equity? Alternately, how conservative should I be, and how much should I keep in a savings account?" The answers to these questions depend heavily on the time horizon of a particular investment

A time horizon is, in simplest terms, the estimated length of time over which an investment will be maintained before being liquidated or sold. Determining your time horizon is essential for deciding which types of investment vehicles will be included in your portfolio. Risk assessment and asset allocation are two factors heavily informed by your time horizon. Once we understand your time horizon, desired risk exposure, and income needs, we can get to work selecting investments.

The Emergency Fund

In order to illustrate this dynamic, let's use something I call an "emergency fund" as an example. Just like its name implies, the emergency fund is there to try to cover any of life's unanticipated financial burdens—catastrophic situations of all shapes and sizes. These could include unplanned-for medical expenses, unexpected layoffs, or that leaky roof that morphed into a $10,000 project overnight. Perhaps you're a freelancer and are "between jobs" at the moment, but you still need to cover living expenses.

Enter your emergency fund. Think of it as your safety net, the wide expanse of springy fabric they spread beneath an acrobat at the circus. Your emergency fund helps you to survive while you get back on your feet. If you have one, there's probably no need to panic when things go awry—as long as the funds are available when disaster comes a-calling.

I want to emphasize here: *as long as the funds are available*. I don't mean to be overly pessimistic, but we know that these negative situations can arise very quickly. Accordingly, the money in the emergency fund must be available at a moment's notice. It cannot be tied up in investments you aren't allowed to touch, or in vehicles that will punish you severely if you try.

Let's say you've put aside $10,000 in your emergency fund. You have a job as a freelance Internet consultant and rely on your car to get from job to job—in other words, the various tech companies you work for are scattered around the city. One morning on the way to a branding meeting, you get into a high-speed collision that luckily (and miraculously) leaves you unscratched.

Unfortunately for you, your car is not so lucky.

Your car is totaled from the collision. You'll lose your job if you can't get to work, and you rely on your car to get to and from work. You need to dip into your emergency fund to find a new car, and fast.

Here's the good news: you're one of my clients. You'll have the money you need to purchase a new car because we've made sure your emergency fund is invested only in low-risk liquid assets such as money markets. Investments such as these can usually be converted rapidly into cash. Because emergencies don't usually come with a courtesy notice months in advance, we steered clear of tying up your emergency fund in long-term investments such as real estate. That way, when you needed the money, it was ready and available.

How Long Is Your Horizon?

The trick to understanding time horizons is simply matching the appropriate vehicle investments with your goals and objectives. Generally, we can divide these goals into three buckets: short-term, intermediate, and long-term. I consider short-term goals to be those that focus roughly on the next three years. Intermediate goals fall between three and five years. Long-term goals are closer to the ten-year range.

With short-term goals—and thus short-term horizons—we need to be less aggressive than we can be with long-term goals. One short-term goal might be saving up for an impending marriage. Say you come to me expecting to be married to your long-time girlfriend within the next two to three years. You anticipate that you will need an outlay of cash—not just for wedding expenses, but also to help you and your wife begin your new life together.

So we craft an investment strategy that is not too hazardous. We need to reduce the risk of loss by relying on cash or cash-like investment vehicles. We look toward money market funds and short-term certificates of deposit. The conservative strategy matches your short time horizon. We anticipate well, as your marriage takes place at the end of the following year, and you have the cash to pay for your expenses. How many newlyweds can say that?

Now, if we had placed your money in high-risk investments and the market had dropped, you would have likely needed to pull the money before the investment had a chance to recover from the loss. The peaks and valleys of the stock market would have simply been too dangerous for your needs. You knew you'd need the cash in the immediate future; that was non-negotiable. If a valley had occurred at the wrong time—say, right when you and your wife were writing the check for the gorgeous outdoor gardens where you had your wedding reception—you would have been out of luck.

Understanding time horizons also gives you the confidence not to overreact when the stock market does take a dip—as it inevitably will. In the fall of 2008, we experienced a significant market drop that scared many individuals into abandoning their long-term strategies. People panicked. Countless American citizens shifted their portfolios away from aggressive mixtures of investments into solely conservative investments. They cut their losses when the market was at its worst, pulling cash out of the stock market and stuffing it into low-risk vehicles—and losing a staggering portion of their wealth along the way.

The outcome could have been much happier had these individuals realized that their money had a long-term horizon, with long-term goals. If the investments hurt by the market drop were those put aside for retirement in a few decades, for example, these individuals would have likely benefited greatly from a bit of patience. Had they left the money in place in 2008, all of their losses would have probably been recovered by 2014—and then some.

You might be wondering why we ever consider risky investments in the first place if safer alternatives exist. The answer is deceptively simple. Generally speaking, the higher the risk, the greater the reward. When they have the appropriate time horizon to incorporate higher-risk investment vehicles, I urge clients to do so. Using a mixture of investments with varying risk can lead to impressive gains. It's all about knowing when to use which strategy. As the saying goes, timing is everything.

Here's what I consider having long-term goals. Let's say you're twenty-three years old and want to put money away for at least the next ten years. You want to save up for a down payment on a house, and maybe you hope to be married with kids someday. But you believe these things are far in the future, around the decade-mark.

Your long-term horizon allows us to take more risk. We've got seven years until you hit thirty. Consequently, we're not going to lean heavily on short-term strategies such as a money market account or short-term bonds. We can be moderately aggressive with your portfolio, striking an appropriate balance. The stock market's peaks and valleys are less scary for your portfolio, since the long horizon allows for many cycles of the market without any pressing need to withdraw funds.

Isn't it nice to be young?

Starting Young

Long-term horizons open the doors for a multitude of investment opportunities that can result in huge gains over a lifetime of investing. There is an undeniable advantage to starting young. Adopting a financial plan in your twenties or thirties helps ensure good financial habits and good investments that will mount over a long career. When you start young, time is on your side. Your portfolio has time to recover from any dips in the market or investment mishaps.

One of the most important advantages to starting young has to do with insurance planning. Obtaining life insurance is much easier when you're young and healthy. Complications become more likely to arise the longer you hold off on insurance planning.

The problem is: what young person wants to think about life insurance? Death seems like a far-off planet in a distant solar system. Believe me, I understand that prioritizing long-term savings for insurance or retirement can be difficult for a young person. For many, the idea of doing retirement planning at a young age is like handing over hard-earned money to an old stranger they've never met. You're working hard in your twenties and thirties, with many pressing responsibilities and concerns. The common financial goals I see among this age group include saving for things like grad school, a wedding, and having a baby.

Still, I encourage my young clients to take a long-term view. There is no better time to start saving than now. And if they've got their eyes on getting married and starting a family, that's all the more reason to adopt a long-term view. It isn't just they who stand to benefit from saving—it's their kids and grandkids, too. I like to think that when these clients reach retirement in thirty or forty years, they'll thank their younger selves for their foresight.

On Depreciation

One thing we do need to take into account with long-term goals is depreciation. Long-term investments are usually subject to depreciation due to inflation and taxation—and neither of those should make you want to pop the champagne.

Let's consider a 401(k) plan for your retirement. The 401(k) plan will likely have a very long time horizon. If over ten years, your retirement investments only have an average return of 1 percent, you actually might have *lost* money. When we consider various taxes on the account, and that the historic annual inflation rate is around 3 percent, your investment will have depreciated in value.

For this reason, I joke sometimes that certificates of deposit—financial products with typically very low interest rates—should actually be called certificates of depreciation. In order to avoid losing money, we must match your long-term goals with investment vehicles likely to yield on average, say, 8 percent. If you're only making 1 or 2 percent, you'll lose money.

Approaching Retirement

Many people in their forties, fifties, and sixties come to see me, fearful that they haven't saved enough over their lifetimes. They're worried they have been too busy earning money to think about investing it properly. They feel they've missed the boat on putting into action any multifaceted financial plan.

They come to me, worried and burdened, and I tell them, "You're in the right place! You're doing exactly what you should be doing." I cannot stress this enough: *it's never too late to formulate a plan.* We can't change the past, so the time to get started is now.

Let's say you come to me in the last five years of your life. You might fear it is too late to make much of a difference in your finances, but you attended my seminar and you're convinced there is hope for your accounts. We grow your money, and when you pass away, you're able to transfer your increased funds to your two favorite nieces.

It really is never too late. If you're a bit younger, in your fifties or sixties and approaching retirement, understanding time horizons is equally important for you as for younger investors. If a client comes to me at age sixty, planning to retire in five years, he's still got plenty of time! If the average life expectancy hovers around eighty-five, his horizon is *twenty-five* years. After retirement, he'll be around for a while. And he'll need money to live. Whether he chooses to spend his retirement traveling the globe, working a part-time job at a hardware store, or visiting his grandkids in Illinois, that money is going to have to last him a while. It's our job to make sure it does.

It's true that, as we age, we have less time to recover from past mistakes, or from circumstances completely beyond our control. If you were in your late fifties in 2008 and your portfolio took a hit when the market crashed, that money naturally has less time to recover than if you'd been thirty-three when the economy tanked. No one said life was fair.

But if you were to take your portfolio to us at sixty-four, we could still make a big difference in your financial future.

It's essential that we have a strategy to grow your money, beat inflation and taxation, and beat longevity risk. You could live another thirty years—more power to you—which means it's not at all too late to make sure your money will support you in the life you want to live.

People forget how lengthy retirement can be. I work to help make sure my clients will never run out of money after they exit the workforce, whether they live to be sixty-five or a hundred. We can't do that without a solid game plan that takes into account the volatility of the market and those all-important factors—inflation, taxation, and longevity. When we plan with those considerations in mind, we can almost see into the future. We may not be able to see exactly what will happen and when, but we can help ensure that, no matter what happens, it won't wreak havoc on your finances or your life.

STRATEGY #3

Preserve Your Investments

This third strategy is a delicate yet crucial one for my clients to understand. Now that you are familiar with time horizons, I hope you agree that in order to beat inflation and taxation, you should have some equity exposure, or a percentage of your portfolio invested in stocks. This becomes proportionately safer the longer the time horizon is—if you have forty years to meet your financial goals, it's a much safer bet than if you have, say, four. But it is fair to say that, in the long term, the best assurance that you'll have a return on your money may very well be to have a chunk of your money invested in the stock market.

Now, here's where it gets tricky. Remember the emergency fund? The namesake of that fund—*the emergency*—is by definition unexpected. In Strategy #2, we talked about the kinds of personal emergencies we all face in our lives: car wrecks, health scares, lost jobs, and so on. These are the storms every human being has weathered at one point or another. But emergencies can also come in much stronger gales, from forces in the outside world.

These emergencies can hit at anytime, sinking the market. If you don't preserve your investments, then you are at the mercy of the market. You have no recourse—you're David going naked up against Goliath. If a natural disaster, terrorist attack, political turmoil, or random catastrophe occurred tomorrow and threatened global markets, you'd stand to lose a substantial percentage of your life savings.

And yet, at the other end of the spectrum, we have established that it isn't wise to simply opt out of equity exposure altogether for fear of another disaster like September 11, 2001, even though this disaster had catastrophic effects on the market. When properly balanced to help manage risk, portfolios can benefit wildly from stock gains. The challenge, then, is to maintain that delicate balance. How can we be actively invested in the stock market and yet have some kind of preservation strategy for these investments? How do we mitigate and manage the risk we're engaging in?

Striking the Suitable Balance

Some conservative financial advisors disparage the stock market and warn their clients not to tangle with the ravenous wolves of Wall Street. But avoiding the stock market altogether is not a risk management strategy I encourage my clients to engage in. In doing so, you're almost taking a negative return in exchange for giving up all the potential positive returns! If you define "risk" as "losing your hard-earned money," then you haven't avoided risk at all. You may actually be *losing money* by refusing to play.

This is where understanding time horizons comes into play. If we remember that over time, the market is probably going to do better, that the successive peaks will be higher than the valleys, we realize that opting out of the market for long-term investing would lose us money. And that's not what any of us want.

If opting out isn't a risk management strategy, then we must acknowledge that our investment in the stock market is an asset like any other. What do we do with our most vital assets, such as our lives, our health, and our homes? We protect them. We have homeowners insurance to protect against fires and floods. We have car insurance in case our car gets into a wreck. We have health insurance to protect ourselves from unforeseen medical costs or debilitating illnesses. Having insurance in each of these areas is our way of saying: "These things are important to me. They have intrinsic value."

For many people, their biggest material asset is their retirement portfolio. Your retirement savings probably have a net worth far greater than that of your car, maybe even your house. And yet, when I look at a new client's portfolio and ask, "Where's your insurance?" they look at me like I'm crazy! It would never occur to them not to have insurance on their life, home, or car—but they cannot fathom why on earth they would need it on their portfolio.

It's a huge gap in thinking, one I've seen time and time again. In the same vein as our health or homes, *our investments must be preserved.* If we have insurance on all the other things we value so highly, why would we not have insurance on significant assets such as our IRAs?

I urge clients to adopt an intelligent risk management strategy, basically a safety net. Hedge funds do what their name implies—hedging—in order to manage their risk. This is a complex form of risk management that requires a lot of learning and work. And one of the most cost-efficient preservation strategies an individual (as opposed to a larger entity such as a hedge fund) can pursue is a fixed annuity. This is why I believe fixed annuities are among the best options to meet personal needs for risk management—an option that is unfortunately often overlooked.

So What's an Annuity?

An annuity is a financial insurance product that mitigates risk. I recommend it to those who seek a guaranteed steady income stream as part of their retirement strategy, and who want a degree of certainty that their money will last.

Like any financial product, there are distinct pluses and minuses to annuities. For one, the insurance you're getting is not free. The insurance expense normally runs between 1 and 2.5 percent. Here's where I love to tell my clients, "In the absence of value, price is irrelevant." I tell them this to remind them that if you believe that the value of the protection of an annuity is necessary, than that 2 percent fee you pay is well worth it. Again, you're paying for protection. You're insuring one of your most valuable assets, the one you've spent a life-time working to accrue.

It's also important to remember that the annuity is a long-term investment option subject to the claim-fulfilling ability and the financial viability of the major insurance company issuing it. Unlike people, not all annuities are created equal.

The annuity works fairly simply. You make an initial investment into one, and it then makes a series of future payments to you. You can divide up these payments in various ways. The size of each is affected by the cost and length of the payment period.

Let's say you are living as a widow and you're worried about money. Here's where the annuity comes in. If your spouse had purchased one twenty years ago, making an initial investment of $100,000, this would help ensure that you were well provided for. Once you turn the annuity "on," the insurance company starts making payments directly to you. Based on that initial $100,000 investment, you can choose how you want to divide up those payments. All you have to do is sit back and let the annuity do its work.

Types of Annuities

There are a few different types of annuities I want to discuss: the traditional fixed annuity, the immediate annuity, and the fixed indexed annuity[3]. I recommend certain types depending on my client's individual circumstances and what they are going to use the annuity for. Many factors play in to my decision to recommend one annuity over another.

The primary purpose of these annuities is to guarantee that you will never run out of money. The insurance company issuing such an annuity makes this guarantee. It's almost as if you are guaranteed a paycheck for life.

---

3 Equity Indexed Annuities (EIA, also known as Fixed Index Annuities - FIA) are tax deferred products; they are not tax free. When withdrawals are made from an EIA - the portion of the withdrawal that is not principal will be taxed at applicable income tax rates. Premature distributions (before age 59 1/2) may be subject to an IRS penalty of 10%, in addition to applicable income taxes. If receiving a bonus with an EIA purchase, you may incur higher surrender charges and be subject to a longer surrender period. Tax-qualified assets (e.g. IRA or Roth IRA assets) in EIA's may not be eligible for additional tax benefits. Investors should have adequate resources to cover liquidity needs. EIA's are not: a deposit of any bank; FDIC insured; insured by any federal government agency; or guaranteed by any bank or savings association. Riders and guarantees may be available at additional cost and may not be available in all States. Guarantees are based on the claims paying ability of the issuing company.

A group of my clients went with a fixed indexed annuity in the years before that market drop in 2008. Their principal was guaranteed by the insurance company, as was their income. They were in far better shape than those without such protection who were forced to go back to work in the midst of the recession.

An annuity isn't right for everyone, but it is a financial product I strongly recommend to many of my clients. For some, it can be a complete game-changer. I've seen clients go from feeling uncertain to securing a paycheck for life.

STRATEGY #4

Understand Taxation

When it comes to taxes, I tell my clients, "It's not what you make; it's what you keep." Think about it: there are only so many hours in a day, days in a week, and weeks in a year. You work hard for most of that time to bring home a paycheck you're proud of. You prioritize wisely, keeping your expenses in check and planning for the future. The last thing you need is to give away any more of your precious, hard-earned money than you absolutely have to.

Let's say you are a family lawyer. You earn $100,000 a year, but over 50 percent of your money goes to taxes. Between federal, state, and city taxes, you feel like you are working from January to June for the IRS. Half your earnings, half your year—it all goes to the government hotshots sitting behind a desk somewhere. It's only in July that you begin to make money you'll actually see (never mind get to spend).

No matter how hard you work, without the correct tax avoidance strategies, your income will seem deflated. The tax impact is too severe.

We want to help ensure that you keep as much of your earnings as possible. The levels of taxation your income and investments are subject to can drastically affect your year-end balance sheet. Our goal is tax diversification, or the implementation of a series of advantageous investments that carry different tax benefits.

Tax Avoidance vs. Tax Evasion

When it comes to taxes, it's very important to understand the difference between two terms: tax avoidance and tax evasion. The former is a set of strategies we can deploy to lessen the burden of taxes you pay to the local, state, and federal governments. There's nothing wrong with tax avoidance—in fact, you should think of it as your new best friend. I find the majority of people who come to me are technically overpaying in one way or another, and they are delighted when we find opportunities for them to avoid these unnecessary taxes.

This is a far cry from tax evasion, which is against the law. Setting up an offshore bank account is just one example of a tax evasion practice, the kind that could land you in prison. In no way do I endorse tax evasion, and if you have an advisor or planner who does, I'd caution you to run as fast as possible in the opposite direction.

Three Types of Money

To get started thinking about tax avoidance, we can view our money as divided into three buckets. The first is **taxable money**, the second is **tax-deferred money**, and the final is **tax-free money**. Taxable money is just what its name implies: taxable. The majority—but not all—of our income is taxable. Think of money as taxable unless you are otherwise notified. It might be money you have sitting in a CD (certificate of deposit) in the bank, in a non-qualified account.

Tax-deferred money is earnings on investments that accumulate without being taxed—until you withdraw the money from an account. Basically, tax-deferred money delays the time at which you pay up. The most familiar tax-deferred investments are individual retirement accounts (IRAs) and deferred annuities. Tax-deferred investments mean tax-free growth. We pay the tax later on, usually once we are earning less than we did in the prime of our career. Thus, when the money is withdrawn, we may be in a lower tax bracket, and the money that grew unencumbered by taxes will now be subjected to a lower rate.

Finally, we have tax-free money. This is money generally exempt from taxes, just as the name implies. Municipal bonds, life insurance proceeds, and 529 education savings plans are all examples of tax-free investment vehicles. These plans can vary by state, tax bracket, and income. Other kinds of money considered tax-free are child support payments, gifts and inheritances, welfare benefits, physical injury damage awards, and cash rebates on purchased items. Reimbursements for adoption expenses are sometimes tax-exempt too, as are monies awarded for educational scholarships.

Once we know the three different types of money, we see that our goal is to shift as much of our taxable money as possible into the tax-deferred or tax-free categories. How do we do this? Well first, legally! All joking aside, we have a number of useful strategies that can maximize our tax-deferred and tax-exempt money. My thinking on smart taxes has been greatly shaped by CPA Ed Slott, author of *The Retirement Savings Time Bomb ... and How to Defuse It*. Ed recommends handy solutions for lessening the draining effect of excessive taxation on our nest eggs.[4]

---

4 Disclosure: Municipal bonds generate tax-free income, and therefore pay lower interest rates than taxable bonds. Therefore, municipal bonds may not be suitable for all investors. Please see your tax professional prior to investing.

A 529 plan is a college savings plan that allows individuals to save for college on a tax-advantaged basis. Every state offers at least one 529 plan. Before buying a 529 plan, you should inquire about the

Converting to the Roth IRA

Often, I advise clients to convert their traditional IRAs to Roth IRAs. Now, you'll have to pay an income tax for this conversion, but your IRA is growing year by year. Think of it as if you were a farmer, with seeds you've recently planted. You'll water them and care for them, making sure they receive the nutrients they need to grow into a lush harvest. Wouldn't you rather pay tax on the seeds when they are smaller than pay taxes on the full harvest?

Traditional IRAs allow you to save pre-tax money, and your earnings grow tax-deferred until you withdraw money during retirement. There are variables that affect this, of course, such as age, or income tax rates at the time of retirement. But once an IRA is converted to a Roth IRA, it can be tax-free forever. Your deposits into a Roth IRA are always tax-deductible. Most important, any withdrawals made from a Roth IRA during retirement are tax-free money. This is largely beneficial when you consider the possible increase in income tax over the years. While we mentioned the need to

---

particular plan and its fees and expenses. You should also consider that certain states offer tax benefits and fee savings to in-state residents. Whether a state tax deduction and/or application fee savings are available depends on your state of residence. For tax advice, consult your tax professional. Non-qualifying distribution earnings are taxable and subject to a 10% tax penalty.

pay income tax on any previously non-taxed balance that is being switched to the Roth IRA, there may be an advantage in the long run. [5]

The Defined Benefit Pension Plan

Another strategy traditionally used by higher earners is to contribute to a defined benefit pension plan. Such a pension plan is enacted by an employer and ensures a monthly payout upon retirement. The size of the payout is determined by your salary and length of employment. Say you earn a healthy income as a general physician with your own practice, and you set up a defined benefit plan a few years ago. You are now able to grow your money tax-deferred and have various tax deductions that lower the percentage of your taxable money. The beauty of such deductions is that your tax bracket is lowered due to these write-offs.

Additionally, we actually included your life insurance policy within the defined benefit plan. That way, the cash

---

5 Disclosure: A Roth IRA distribution is qualified if you've had the account for at least five years and/or the distribution is made after you've reached age 59½, because of your total and permanent disability, in the event of your death, or for first-time homebuyer expenses. Distributions made prior to age 59½ may be subject to a federal income tax penalty. If you convert a traditional IRA to a Roth IRA, you will owe ordinary income taxes on any previously deducted traditional IRA contributions and on all earnings. I suggest that you discuss tax issues with a qualified tax advisor.

value of your life insurance policy could be available in addition to your emergency fund. If this situation were to change dramatically, the cash could be taken out via the loan aspect of the policy, which becomes tax-free.[6]

For Entrepreneurs

If you are working as an entrepreneur in the eyes of the IRS—that is, you are a non-W2 employee or an independent contractor—you have another tax minimization strategy at your disposable. Taxation in this country works generally more in your favor than it does a salaried W2 employee, whose taxes are automatically and routinely deducted from each paycheck. As an independent contractor, you have far more flexibility in using the tax code to your advantage.

There are all kinds of legal tax deductions you are afforded as a businessperson. Many of these are hiding in plain sight—deductions that most likely apply to you, but you simply haven't realized are costing you money. That is, until you write them off as you should! A perfect example might be your vehicle. You work as a freelancer traveling to the homes of your clients. You can deduct a percentage of the cost of operating your

---

6 Disclosure: There are several choices investors have when rolling money over from one plan to another. Since each choice has its own implications, it is recommended that you discuss and compare all potential fees, expenses, commissions, taxes, and legal ramifications with your qualified advisor before making a rollover decision.

car (the percentage used for transportation for business purposes). The same goes for your office furniture and the space in your home you use exclusively for conducting business (this ends up being a percentage of the total square footage). These are all legitimate business write-offs.

It is also usually significantly easier to design a retirement plan when you're an entrepreneur. If you're a salaried W2 employee, you cannot establish a defined benefit plan because you are not your own employer. But as an independent contractor, you are your own boss. You can enact your own defined benefit plan, possibly putting much more money into your retirement plan, and as a result often having much higher tax deductions than your salaried W2 counterparts.

This can make a big difference in savings. We're not just talking about saving a few hundred dollars here and there. We are talking about thousands of dollars of money saved—your hard-earned money going back in your pocket instead of being sent off to the IRS. The difference this makes for my clients is often tremendous. I've had people come to see me, griping that they have "sprung a leak," and are losing a sizable portion of their income to the government every year. Twelve or eighteen months later, they cannot believe how successfully they've been able to stanch the flow.

I use these techniques constantly in my practice. When clients come to me with bona fide businesses they are running—moneymaking businesses, not just shells to hide from the IRS—I recommend they set up consulting or otherwise entrepreneurial ventures. Often, all they need is the encouragement. Once they see that this step works in their favor from a tax point of view, they're sold.

Again, I want to stress that I do not promote or endorse tax evasion strategies of any kind. No amount of money is worth breaking the law and endangering yourself and your family. I'm simply talking about *tax avoidance*, a series of completely above-the-board strategies to help you hold on to as much of your income as you can. If you've never looked into these strategies before, why not start now? The difference it can make in your life is extraordinary.[7]

---

7 Stephen Ng Financial Group, LLC does not offer legal or tax advice. Please consult the appropriate professional regarding your individual circumstance.

To ensure compliance with requirements imposed by the IRS under Circular 230, we inform you that any U.S. Federal tax advice contained in this communication, unless otherwise specifically stated, was not intended or written to be used, and cannot be used, for the purpose of (1) avoiding penalties under the Internal Revenue Code or (2) promoting, marketing, or recommending to another party any matters addressed herein.

Educate Yourself

My average client has a full schedule: a demanding job, a fulfilling family life, and barely enough time left over to eke out a morning jog or catch their favorite TV show after a busy weekend. I understand as much as anyone—any time left goes to the fun stuff. It's often said that people spend more time planning their next vacation, or researching and deciding which new car to buy, than they do planning their retirement. In my experience, this is certainly true.

But that doesn't mean it is wise or prudent to continue putting off retirement planning. Though the list of distractions and legitimate excuses is long and varied, the dangers of failing to educate yourself in financial planning are just as numerous.

Consider the steps you would take as a consumer to educate yourself about the marketplace when buying appliances for a new home. You might visit ConsumerReports.com, check out reviews in magazines or online marketplaces, and even test out the items in question. Certainly, you'd shop around to find the best price once you'd zeroed in on a refrigerator or washing machine.

Similarly, when contemplating our financial futures, we must take steps to understand the marketplace and its many moving parts. The world of finance is not a simple one. Investments are complex, as is the nature of financial planning. The sheer volume of information on the subject is overwhelming. Even the stock market tickers running at the bottoms of our television screens impart a feeling of anxiety to some of my clients.

Many people come to me after having taken a good-natured stab at understanding this confusing field on their own. After trying to learn the basics with a few Google searches, they have often had enough. We joke that they have gotten a case of situational paralysis by analysis. It's just too vast a subject to master in the hours after work, or before the kids wake up.

While all knowledge is good, there is a difficult balance to strike. Even how to find the right sources of information is a mystery. Luckily, I can streamline the process for my clients, narrowing our focus to the portions that are useful to my clients and specifically applicable to their unique financial situations.

When a client comes to me having adopted a strategy already, I always begin by asking what their purpose is. "Why are you using this technique?" I ask. Very often, there's no concrete answer. It's easy to receive one-sided information about an investment vehicle, or to see only the benefits of a retirement plan. I want us to work exclusively with complete, clear, and honest appraisals of every strategy we undertake.

We need to understand the balance of any product or strategy's benefits and costs. We must know its pluses and minuses. This is an ironclad rule of mine. As an independent advisor, I deal with multiple strategies and companies, not only one. I try to create clarity for my clients daily.

Arming Yourself

I encourage my clients to arm themselves with information about the financial world. I recommend reading the financial or market-based sections of any quality publication as frequently as possible. Start small, perusing *Barron's* or *Investor's Business Daily* when you have the chance. Any knowledge can help you to understand the market and the options available to you as you plan for the future.

Of course the media bombards each of us in our daily lives. Financial news shows can be useful tools without a doubt—if used carefully. Whatever we hear, we want to be sure to check it out on our own, or with an advisor. Some of the views shared on the financial talk shows can be self-serving. As in all areas in life, it's important not to take any piece of information and consider it in a vacuum. Balance, again, is the key.

As they learn, some of my clients come to realize they have a passion for a particular area of financial planning. They become engaged with the material as they undertake a course of informal study whenever their schedules allow. Clients like these will often come to me with a list of financial products they've read about, inquiring as to which will be the best option for their financial situation. I'm happy to serve as an advisor, sharing my years of experience in the field to help them navigate through strategies, options, and best practices.

It's no different than a home medical diagnosis via WebMD. If you have an ache or pain, you'll go to the Internet and learn more about it. You might have a general idea of what could be wrong, but ultimately, you'll visit a physician. You've done your homework, so you understand what the physician is talking about when he references MRIs, x-rays, and various blood tests. You'll let him determine the best course of action. If it's surgery, you won't perform it on yourself—at least, I hope you won't! You'll visit a specialist and share the diagnosis. If it's medication, you won't self-prescribe. You'll look to your doctor to do that for you.

The same dynamic is at work between my clients and me. It's easier for you to feel confident in your plan if you have a basic understanding of the terms and products we'll be looking at. You've educated yourself enough that you can process the information we'll be utilizing to your advantage. Together, we'll pool our knowledge and formulate a prudent plan.

Beware the Hype

When learning about financial markets, I urge my clients to resist being controlled by the headlines. Television networks are in business to keep people watching, and newspapers to keep people reading—so the media conglomerates and publishing giants are prone to sensationalist stories with overly emotional coverage. Clients will come to me saying they need to sell everything, fearful of the market dropping dramatically because an exaggerated headline has convinced them that some new piece of legislation will destroy the economy.

Earlier we discussed having a solid understanding of time horizons; this is where that understanding comes into effect. I remind my clients to sit tight when the market dips. They are well diversified, and a valley of any size is the wrong time to sell. If you have a ten-year horizon, there's no need to over-react to the natural cycles of the market and sell due to panic.

On the flip side: beware of falling into a trap promoting a specific company or industry as the hot new sector to invest in. Such hype leads to bubbles in certain fields, and the news coverage produces scores of over-confident investors looking to buy. Alan Greenspan calls it "irrational exuberance," and others call it the feeding frenzy. When you were growing up, your teachers called it herd mentality. Whatever the name, the message is loud and urgent: buy, buy, buy.

Those who listen are convinced that everything that goes up in the economy will only continue to rise higher and higher. But you know better. Be wary of any advice that sounds too good to be true. Do not fall prey to the emotion that drives the press and the herd, be it greed or fear. These are the emotions that can lead your smart investment strategy astray. Overcome the tendency to act on the last piece of information you heard on the news, and your bank account will thank you down the line.

One Size Doesn't Fit All

As you begin to learn more about investment planning, you'll find so-called experts all around you. People you previously thought of as fitness trainers, dentists, or painters might rush to provide you with financial advice. Kind souls will share with you what they've learned in their own investment quests, tipping you off to a hot stock or a fund with high returns.

Be polite in receiving such advice, but also be careful not to adopt wholesale the particular plan of a friend. It might be working for him or her, but everyone's finances are different. Just like in football, the game plan that works for one offensive team might not work for another. One team has a quarterback with a strong arm and a fast wide receiver. The other team might have a quarterback who has a weak arm but runs unusually well, with guards who can block the opposing defense for him. Each team needs its own book of plays.

To return to our physician example, the course of treatment that works for one patient might not work for another. Every body is its own intricate organism, needing different medication and care. So, too, do you need your own financial plan. One strategy, one stock, or one mutual fund may be suitable for one person but entirely unsuitable for another person's financial goals.

I might recommend a specific course of action to a young professional with at least twenty more years in the workforce. Because his investment horizon is very long, I might recommend that he think about investing heavily in the biotechnology sector. This is an aggressive portion of our investment plan, as the biotech sector is at the forefront of technology and may see vast advancements in the coming years.

This same investment would be unwise for a client in their late sixties or seventies. Such clients are on the distribution side of their financial arc, no longer accumulating money but now dispersing it throughout their retirements. Clients of this age don't have the time horizon the young professional has, and thus the volatility of an investment in the cutting-edge tech sector would make little sense for their portfolios. If the market were to drop, the client in retirement would have little time to recover. But the young professional would have plenty of time, and little to worry about.

This is just one pertinent example of why advice in the financial sectors cannot be one-size-fits-all. Age is not the only factor that affects the financial suitability of recommendations. Differing financial priorities and goals between individuals of the same age could mean your portfolio might look entirely different from that of your twin brother. By nature, your finances are a personal matter unique to you. Recommendations must be suitable to your financial past and present, and they must take into account your own future aims. Your neighbor's plan will do little good for you. Do yourself a financial favor and take all advice in context.

Another word of warning—a sophisticated investor might offer advice on particular stocks. From his point of view, it's advantageous to him to buy and sell a stock on the same day, closing out his position and taking some profit. Without proper instruction, you might be stuck with the stock months later, having misunderstood his tip. Day trading requires experience that is beyond the grasp of most new investors, so be careful when fielding instruction.

Starting from Scratch

A percentage of my clients come to me having never looked into these areas on their own. That's totally fine, and I will take the necessary steps to fill in all the blanks for them. It's my responsibility to share any wisdom I've gathered to guide you. I'll help you understand the fundamentals and the basics—the difference between a stock and a bond, or the different types of risk.

I also offer educational meetings, seminars, and workshops for clients and potential clients. The topics run the gamut on investment and financial planning, giving clients a macro-perspective that includes multiple different strategies. I like to believe that we provide attendees with a view of the forest before they zoom in for a view of the trees.

This broad spectrum of information is an excellent knowledge base; it's also the reason many prospective clients come to see me. They've attended a seminar or a workshop and liked what they heard, so they choose to come in for a free consultation. Together we outline their unique situation—the desires, objectives, and goals that fuel them and dictate their financial choices. At that point, I point out how I can best apply my specific knowledge and expertise to help them, and how our partnership would function to help them fulfill their dreams.

STRATEGY #6

Diversify

You've heard it over and over since grade school—never put all your eggs in one basket. There's a reason this adage is so often repeated: to stake too much on the outcome of just one thing is rarely a wise move, especially when it comes to your finances. An "all eggs in one basket" approach to your investment portfolio would mean placing a large portion of your savings into one stock or one mutual fund. That's not good.

So what does this age-old saying mean when it comes to your finances? Two words: asset allocation.[8]*

The term *asset allocation* refers to a healthy investment portfolio, one well balanced with many different types of proverbial eggs in the basket. Large cap, small cap,

8 Neither asset allocation nor diversification guarantee a profit or protect against a loss in a declining market. They are methods used to help manage investment risk.

international—you name it, the inclusion of many different asset classes makes for a balanced basket. Diversification is one of the most important principles of financial planning. We need to diversify when designing a portfolio, meaning we seek different types of investments. But we also need to diversify for each of your financial goals, employing a variety of strategies to help you reach every target.

How Asset Allocation Can Save Your Neck

You might think, "What's the harm in sticking with one financial product if it's working?" Many people thought the same in the years before 2008. Individuals were overinvested in stocks, without any asset preservation strategy. They didn't diversify with other strategies that protected their risk. With no money allocated to annuities—a fixed indexed annuity, for example, that might have protected their money from market downfall—they lost most of their savings in the fiasco caused by the market drop of 2008.

By contrast, my clients who had diversified with fixed annuities survived that drop because they were well protected across the spectrum of strategies employed. Their monies in the stock market were affected, sure, but their diversification allowed them to ride it out. They knew that in the long term, what was lost would likely come back to them.

This raises the question: is there such a thing as being too safe, or too protected? Certainly. Some individuals overreacted after the market dropped in 2008. In many cases, they moved almost all of their investable assets into money market funds. This is the flip side of the same coin—being massively underexposed is just as harmful as being overexposed when it comes to undiversified portfolios. With a strategy this conservative, the nervous investors missed the past six years of market return and upswing. After factoring in inflation and taxation, this group has actually lost money. The middle road, unsurprisingly, is where the answer lies.

When it comes to investments, I remind my clients that five brains are better than one. While there's nothing wrong with staying within one investment, I prefer to diversify on every level possible. If investing in multiple stocks, I recommend my clients use different combinations of companies. That way, we are diversifying by gaining the expertise of different portfolio managers. We can then reap the benefits of each management team's brainpower, resources, and respective strengths.

Asset Classes

The truly diversified portfolio benefits from smart asset-class selection. What's an asset class? Essentially, an asset class refers to a bunch of investments (or assets) that are grouped by their similarities. They behave similarly in the marketplace, and have comparable investment characteristics, such as level of risk and return.

I try to spread my clients' investments across various asset classes: large cap, small cap, mid cap, high yield, international, and domestic. The most up-to-date theories on financial portfolios recommend having investments in each of these categories. Over time, the broad range of asset allocation recommended by modern portfolio theory usually has the best risk-adjusted rate of return.

Assembling such a diversified portfolio on your own is difficult, but not impossible. It would require many hours of careful research with investment management companies to determine which investment vehicles fit into each asset class. If you knew you needed knee surgery, would you go to medical school and learn the trade for seven years in order to perform it on yourself? Probably not. Similarly, diversification of assets requires a career's worth of insight and experience.

This is where a financial advisor's wisdom is priceless. A trained professional can impart years of study in a single session, and your portfolio tends to reap the benefits.

Dynamic Asset Allocation

Let's say your husband has worked in finance and managed your money for the majority of your life. Unfortunately, he was recently diagnosed with Alzheimer's disease. You don't feel he has the full mental capacity to grapple with this much information any longer, and he has handed over the management of the portfolio to you.

Because he has already sagely diversified the portfolio, my value to you is my ongoing ability to stay on top of the ever-changing market and its different financial products, and to attempt to keep your portfolio balanced and highly diversified as we move forward. Things need to be readjusted to respond to the economy in any given year. The portfolio's asset class mixture often must be rebalanced[9] to respond to trends, the economic times, and the economic forecast.

This story is one of dynamic asset allocation. My strategy in this case would be to rebalance the portfolio so as to bring the asset mix back to its long-term target. I reduce holdings in certain assets and add to holdings in others. My chief goal is to reduce fluctuation risks and help achieve returns that exceed your target benchmarks. This will help see that you are well cared for in your later years.

---

9 Rebalancing can entail transaction costs and tax consequences that should be considered when determining a rebalancing strategy.

A Cursory Review of Correlation

When considering asset allocation, we must correctly analyze the correlation between types of investments. Using historical data, such analysis illustrates how two asset classes respond in relation to the price of one another. This data is presented to us on a fancy-looking chart called a correlation matrix. But don't worry: reading the matrix is more straightforward than it might appear at first glance.

There are three things to remember when it comes to correlation. First, if two asset classes have a correlation of plus one, they are said to be perfectly correlated. Perfectly correlated asset classes then move either up or down in complete synchronization, or in lockstep.

Next, if two asset classes have a correlation of negative one, they are said to be perfectly negatively correlated. Perfectly negatively correlated asset classes move in exactly opposite directions. As one moves up, the other moves down. There is an equal and opposing movement between the two.

Last, if two asset classes have a correlation of zero, they are said to have a random correlation. If two asset classes are randomly correlated, the rise of one could be met with a drop or a fall by the other asset class. A rise and a fall are equally likely.

Now that we understand the three possible correlations between asset types, we must consider how to use correlation to our advantage. Imagine if we had only per-fectly positively correlated asset classes. This would mean that when things go up, *all* of our investments went up, too. Sounds great, doesn't it? But I'm sure you see the potentially disastrous implications here. The dark side is, well ... dark. If things went down in the market, *all* of our investments would tank, too. Every last one.

As tempting as it seems for the optimists among you, we cannot have all of our assets moving in the same direc-tion. Would you bet all of your earnings on a single coin toss? I imagine the great majority of you wouldn't. Thus, negative correlation is essential to a balanced and diversi-fied portfolio.

A final note: correlation between asset classes is not con-stant. If it were, people like Sharon wouldn't need my help! Indeed, correlation changes unpredictably over time. With keen analysis, we might—at best—glean a vague sense of what the correlation between two asset classes might look like years down the road. But this is leaving the health of our portfolio up to chance, no different than if a physician were to cease learning after graduating from medical school and insist on operating today with only the techniques and tools of thirty years ago. As information multiplies and our world changes, we must update our strategies—hence the need for ongoing dynamic asset allocation.

The Efficient Frontier

Now you have a better sense of the guidelines for portfolio diversification, and of course, you know what is at stake. I'm sure you're wondering what the absolute best balance of asset classes is—the perfect ratio between asset types that will result in the greatest growth of your hard-won money. Clients call me and ask, "What's the right mix between stocks and bonds?"

There's an easy answer to that question—slightly more stocks than bonds—and a necessarily more nuanced and complex one. The more complicated answer is that this magic recipe we seek is revealed to us as the *efficient frontier*, a graphic presentation of the various possible portfolios that can be assembled from your set of assets to offer the highest expected rate of return with the lowest level of defined risk.

The graph allows us to play around with the balance of your assets and acquire information before we actually invest. I like to think of the efficient frontier as a test kitchen. Imagine you set out to bake a delicious batch of brownies, but you had no recipe to follow. All you knew were the ingredients you needed: butter, sugar, eggs, flour, cocoa powder, and vanilla extract. You needed to figure out the ratios between these ingredients in order to yield your desired outcome—a yummy dessert.

The endless experimentation in a test kitchen has zero consequences. You can try out the different combinations of your known ingredients until you strike the perfect balance among them. The same goes for balancing assets via the efficient frontier, only when it's numbers you are playing with, there are fewer dirty pots and pans.

The efficient frontier appears on a graph as a curved line, shaped like a boomerang. The line illustrates optimal asset allocation, showing you the portfolios that offer the greatest expected rate of return for a set level of risk. How far you move on the scale of risk is up to you. Below the line are all the hypothetical portfolios that don't maximize your growth for the level of risk to which you are exposed. We don't want you to lose sleep for nothing, right?

The efficient frontier uses historical data to approximate future market behavior. Of course, there is no way for us to actually predict the future market with exact accuracy. If we could, our headaches would be solved!

Short of a miracle, understanding asset classes, the importance of correlation, and the efficient frontier represents the best of today's thinking on asset allocation. And if it's all starting to blur in your head, don't worry. That's where I come in.

STRATEGY #7

Seek Advice

One of my favorite quotations is Proverbs 15:22: "Plans fail for lack of counsel, but with many advisors they succeed." I wholeheartedly agree with this in all areas of life, especially when it comes to finances.

You might assume one financial advisor can handle all of your investment needs. In theory this is possible, and there are certainly professionals who fancy themselves jacks-of-all-trades—men and women with formidable knowledge in multiple areas. But the advisor with your best interest at heart knows that the strongest plan will usually benefit from the input of as many specialists as required. How many specialists you need will of course depend on your unique financial needs, goals, and considerations.

When was the last time you stuck around after a movie to watch the credits roll? As we all know, the list of names is practically endless. On the really big Hollywood blockbusters, you might hear three full songs by the time the credits stop rolling! A movie requires a daunting number of specialists and experts for everything to go off without a hitch.

As a financial planner, I view my role as akin to that of a movie producer. I oversee everything and synthesize the efforts of a bunch of different people. Whereas a producer marshals the talents of the director, actors, crew, assistants, lawyers, caterers, and a thousand others, it is my job to marshal the talents of my colleagues who specialize in areas such as real estate, tax law, eldercare, etc. Like any good producer, I know which department to ask for lighting, and where to go to for sound. Each individual plays his or her part, contributing unique gifts and talents, and together we are able to tell one coherent and beautiful story.

This is the approach I take with my firm. I know when additional specialists are needed. I have an estate-planning attorney, an eldercare attorney, and a host of CPAs with different areas of knowledge and expertise. I want to provide my clients with high-quality advice from every angle, and I know that multiple minds are better than one. The relevant fields within financial planning are so vast that seeking the advice of specialists is not only humble—it is highly advisable. Every one of these foci has become so layered and complex, I'd be a fool to think I could flawlessly navigate them all.

It's true that when many minds are involved, the result is only as strong as the coordination among them. Ask any movie producer: the last thing you need is for your crew to mutiny on the same day your actors start complaining about how the director "doesn't understand them." You want to make sure everyone is working smoothly together, like a well-oiled machine.

That's my job. I take the lead and act as the quarterback, coordinating my team of advisors. And in so doing, we are able to give you the highest, most specialized level of service you could ever want.

The Eldercare Attorney

Since many of my clients are older, one area of focus I've found indispensable is eldercare. My clients tend to reap lasting benefits from the advice of an eldercare attorney who helps them plan for long-term care, especially in the event that they live for an extended period of time and need more assistance than originally anticipated. Usually I recommend that my clients over the age of sixty or sixty-five consider seeking the advice of an eldercare attorney.

Life doesn't always pan out the way we intend it to, and unfortunately, the need for an eldercare attorney's services can come earlier than expected. This past year, a friend of mine, Jim, suffered from a debilitating stroke. Jim was only fifty-four years old, and up until the stroke, he had been pretty healthy. He survived, but he is severely disabled as a result of the stroke. Now Jim requires the around-the-clock care that only a nursing home can provide.

The saddest part is that Jim hadn't done any eldercare planning or considered long-term in any real, tangible way. He figured he was still healthy and fit, and young enough that such planning could be pushed off a few years. Typically, such a delay might have been okay. Sadly for Jim, that delay was a costly mistake that will now affect him for the rest of his life.

Suddenly facing increased health care costs when you no longer have an income to cover them is scary—and it's also a very real possibility. These days, our advanced medical technology means a greatly increased chance of surviving a major medical event such as a heart attack or a stroke. This is of course excellent news, but it does create another set of problems. Now we need to prepare for the possibility of being alive and *unable* to provide for ourselves for years or even decades.

The average cost of long-term care, either at home or in a nursing facility, is staggering—approximately $120,000 per year in most parts of the country. It's frightening math when you consider that you might need such care for, on average, five years. And sometimes it's a lot longer than that.

This is why it can make a world of difference to have an expert on your team. An eldercare attorney attends to exactly these sorts of issues, helping you sail the murky waters before the storm ever hits. Such an attorney might set up a trust to cover unforeseen future expenses, or—if you are already ill or disabled—help you figure out an affordable way to ensure ongoing care. Whether in home care or in a nursing home, such arrangements require the drafting of a thick pile of legal documents, something you don't want to navigate alone.

The CPA

Unless you feel equipped to prepare your own taxes, a CPA (Certified Public Accountant) will prepare your tax return. But the role of a good CPA doesn't end there. The CPA is one of your best resources for advice on how to implement tax avoidance strategies and how to steer clear of tax evasion, as we discussed in Strategy #4. If your CPA is not suggesting ways to make your financial life more efficient, I'd suggest looking elsewhere for one who will.

Your CPA should not just be doing historical record-keeping. He should be working to help grow your money and lessen the taxation on your income. He should be continually shifting as much money as possible from the taxable bucket we mentioned earlier to the tax-deferred bucket. I refer my clients to CPAs who go above and beyond for their clients, making tax strategizing a priority. I can't overstate the difference this can make for a healthy, happy retirement.

The Estate-Planning Attorney

Whereas a CPA understands the intricate minutiae of taxation and tax returns, an estate-planning attorney is the go-to strategist for clients when they consider issues relating to death. While it's never exactly pleasant to visualize our demise, it is something that becomes more and more pressing as we age.

I have many clients who come to me and say, "I want to make sure my money passes to my children as intact as possible. How can we minimize estate and inheritance taxes?"

Enter the estate-planning attorney. This individual can help you structure your estate to minimize these taxes. She will be able to answer every question you may have regarding your estate plan, including but not limited to wills, trusts, probate, healthcare proxy, durable power of attorney, and the overall transfer of ownership of assets in the most efficient way possible. An estate-planning attorney will be responsible for drafting the documents guiding the disbursement of the entirety of a client's estate.

Once they've established an estate plan, I recommend that my clients review all of their legal documents pertaining to estate planning at least once every three years. All sorts of changes can occur over time, particularly relating to beneficiaries.

I also urge you to plan earlier rather than later. Again, this isn't fatalistic; it is simply being judicious about what might happen. No one relishes the thought of death, but it's far worse not to be prepared for the inevitable. And when it comes to potential illness and disabilities that could drastically affect your standard of living, there's really no reason not to have a plan in place.

Think of it this way: the more planning you do now, the easier you'll make it for your family. When I have clients who are hesitant to look into eldercare options or do their estate planning, I remind them that, in all honesty, it isn't for them—it's for the next generation. If not for yourself, then do it for your kids, grandkids, and other family members who will be left alone in their time of loss, wading through all the paperwork you never completed.

I know it's difficult to contemplate, but making such arrangements early on will save you and your loved ones plenty of stress and expense, not to mention the emotional cost of waiting. Like I tell my clients: planning in advance is one of the best gifts you can ever give.

STRATEGY #8

Risk Management Strategies

To live life is to face risk. No matter how hard we try, we cannot totally avoid risk. Even if we stay home and bury our heads in the sand, something could still happen. Our house might catch fire, or the main gas line beneath our street could explode, or there might be a freak tornado that blows our home—and us inside it—to bits.

If we cannot totally avoid it, the question becomes: How do we manage and mitigate risk? That's the question I ask the people who come to my seminars and the clients who walk through my front door.

You've no doubt heard the expression, "The best defense is a strong offense." The saying may be cliché, but the sentiment behind it is profound—especially when it comes to your finances. That one small statement contains the secret formula for managing risk.

In over twenty years of working as a financial planner, I've learned that "the best defense" for my clients usually has three major components: life insurance, disability insurance, and long-term care insurance. There are other types of insurance, too—auto insurance, homeowners, et cetera—but these are the three I will be focusing on here.

In the following pages, we will discuss these three strategies in detail, including why they are essential to your financial health and well-being. Think of them as the linebacker, tackle, and cornerback of your retirement plan. These guys are your defensive players, the backbone of your risk management strategy—and they're going on offense to make sure you and your money are protected.

Life Insurance: Your Linebacker

In football, the middle linebacker is often referred to as the "quarterback of the defense." He is frequently the primary defensive play-caller, and he must react to a wide variety of situations, giving him a key role in the game. This is why I've dubbed life insurance "the linebacker" for your financial defense—because it, too, plays a key role, providing a wide variety of perks.

There are many different types of life insurance. In the same way that there are two main types of linebackers on a football team—outside and middle—there are two main types of insurance: term insurance and cash value life insurance. But did you know that there are multiple types of insurance *within* these two groups?

Term insurance, for example, might cover you for a five-, ten-, fifteen-, twenty-, or even thirty-year term. There are multiple types of cash value policies, too. You've got universal life, adjustable life, whole life, variable universal life, and indexed universal life. So there are essentially five unique types of cash value policies, and they are all different in terms of coverage, cash value, and how that cash value is going to grow.

Most people do not understand the differences among the various types of life insurance, and when they do purchase a policy, they often make mistakes. Mistakes in life insurance can be deadly—no pun intended. All too often I have seen a severe mismatch between a specific product and a person's unique life insurance needs. Remember: life insurance is a long-term vehicle. If you do not have an expert to help you navigate the dizzying array of choices, it becomes crucial that you do due diligence and educate yourself.

Let's say you want a life insurance policy to cover your mortgage. That's all you want—yours is a very specific, tangible need. You are sixty-seven years old and have a fifteen-year mortgage; you want to cover it in case you die before you've paid it off. Most likely, all you need is fifteen-year term insurance. You probably do not need a cash value life insurance policy.

But your financial planner gets a juicy kickback for selling cash value policies. So he talks you into getting universal life insurance instead. You can't really tell the difference—you just go where your guy leads you.

If you had come in to see me, I would have matched you with term insurance for fifteen years—no more, no less. My goal is to match the correct product with a person's particular need. In your case, you had a very specific life insurance need, leading to a very specific solution. By matching you with the correct type of life insurance, I can help ensure that your financial plan is rock solid. And it certainly makes you happy, because now you can rest easy at night, knowing your wife and kids won't be on the hook to pay the mortgage if something happens to you.

Like I always tell my clients: Homeowners insurance is mandated by your bank, auto insurance is mandated by the state, and life insurance is mandated by your love for your loved ones. If you love the people who will be left behind after you're gone, you'll get life insurance.

The Power of Life Insurance

People ask me all the time, "Stephen, do I really need life insurance?" Many people don't understand the point.

The fundamental purpose of life insurance is, number one: to make sure you are mitigating the financial risk when you pass away. But the number two reason is the one we discussed in Strategy #4: you can actually use the cash value as a way to take money out via a loan, *for use during your lifetime.* In other words, life insurance isn't just for once your life is over; you can use it, too. And that is powerful.

In my twenty-two years in practice, I have sold well over a thousand life insurance policies. I've seen things you would not believe. Let's say I have a client with a life insurance policy who commits suicide. All life insurance policies have a suicide clause that's usually two years, meaning if you commit suicide within two years, the insurance company will not pay. After years of battling depression, this client commits suicide in the eighteen month. Though the client had worked hard to buy the policy for his family, wanting them to be provided for, because of the clause, they will never see that money.

I tell this story as a cautionary tale. You should always look into the provisions of your life insurance policy. But I've also seen life insurance do exactly what it was intended to do. You just never know what's going to happen. Why not hope for the best and prepare for the worst?

A final word on life insurance: I've seen many people make the mistake of owning their life insurance policy. "But Stephen," you say, "Isn't that the whole point?" Actually, it isn't. There are three major components of every life insurance contract: the owner, the insured, and the beneficiaries.

Most people assume the owner and the insured are the same person.

But here's the problem: if you have estate tax exposure, that's not good. Though your death benefit may be income-tax free when you pass away, it is not generally estate-tax free. The computation will actually likely *increase* the taxation on your estate.

One solution is to set up an ILIT, or irrevocable life insurance trust. This allows you to have another person own the policy, someone other than you.

Let's say a successful novelist has a $5 million life insurance policy. In this particular case, he is the insured and his wife is the beneficiary. But then he is in a tragic auto accident and passes away. The $5 million death benefit, which is income tax free, is not estate tax free. If he is also the owner of that policy, it means the $5 million is going to be added to his house, car, jewelry, business, book royalties—everything. The government will include that as the overall basis of taxation at the estate tax, federal, and state levels.

But if the novelist had set up an ILIT, he might have avoided this scenario entirely. The irrevocable life insurance trust allows him to make someone else the owner of the policy—his son or daughter, perhaps. That way, if something happens to him, his wife and children are provided for, without the government double dipping from the money he's left behind.

Disability Insurance: Your Tackle

The second tool in risk management is disability insurance. I joke that it's like having a defensive tackle, because you very well might need disability if you get tackled the wrong way!

In the insurance world, the probability of being disabled is called "mobility" as opposed to "mortality"—and it happens more often than people think. I'm not talking about short-term disability, where you take thirty or ninety days off because of a pulled muscle in your back. I'm talking about people who are still disabled after ninety days.

I know a woman who was a prominent dentist, with a fabulous client roster and an impressive income to match. She was also one of the fittest people I knew at the time— she even taught spinning classes at the local gym. Last summer she was out riding her bike with her two teenage daughters and got hit by a truck. Now she's a quadriplegic. She's only forty-nine and is totally disabled. How is she going to replace her income? Before the accident, she had at least sixteen working years left—that's a lot of income to make up for.

If you don't have the ability to go to work and you've got no other income coming in, where's the income going to come from? You're in trouble.

The people who seem to understand this best are doctors. Almost every single one of my clients who works in medicine has disability insurance. Think about it—if a surgeon cannot use his hands, if his hands are injured or shaking, then his career is essentially finished.

This is where disability insurance proves itself vital. The purpose of disability insurance is to replace your ability to go to work and make an income. My friend who got hit by the truck? If she has disability coverage, her whole situation changes. The insurance policy will match her income as a dentist, meaning she can still fulfill her dream of sending her two girls to college, even if she won't be able to stand and applaud them when they walk across the stage.

Long-Term Care Insurance: Your Cornerback

When a cornerback rushes the runner in a football game, his job is one of containment. He wants to direct the runner, either driving him back to the middle of the field or forcing him out of bounds.

Think of long-term care insurance as your cornerback. It's the third risk management strategy in your arsenal, the one focused on containing your future and the people who will be a part of it. Long-term care insurance gives you the power to ensure that you will be cared for in the way you want to be cared for, with the people you've selected, in the place of your choosing.

People are living longer today than ever. We'll talk more about longevity risk in Strategy #9 but here's the gist: if you have a stroke or get sick and still have many more years to live, who is going to pay for the care you'll need? Most people do not realize that long-term care costs a great deal, whether you choose in-home care or go to a nursing home, which can easily cost $120,000 a year in the U.S. And according to the insurance companies, people need long-term care for an average of five years. If you have Alzheimer's, that number shoots up to fifteen years. The price tag is astronomical.

If you don't have a game plan for long-term care, you are at risk. This is one area that will really deplete your assets. I've seen it happen to too many people, and it's always a night-mare—your investable assets vanish faster than you would believe.

Luckily, there are a number of different solutions right now, whether in insurance or in eldercare planning. If it is within your budget, the most efficient solution is to buy a long-term care insurance policy, and as usual, there are many different types. Some of them are strictly long-term care, some of them are a combination of long-term care and life insurance, and some of them are a combination of long-term care and annuities.

Remember, there are always pluses and minuses to every strategy. Maybe living in Malaysia for their cheaper coverage sounds wonderfully exotic to you. But what if your grandchildren are here? What if all your doctors and medical experts are here? If you're a few thousand miles away, this will be compromised, and it could even result in serious problems down the line as your health begins to fail.

There is no perfect solution; you must always weigh the advantages and disadvantages against what feels right for you. If you are moving to another country because it's your lifelong dream, fantastic. If you are doing it because you have no other choice and you cannot remain here with your family, that's bad—and it can probably be avoided if you have the appropriate insurance policies in place.

The Best Defense Is a Strong Offense

Life insurance, disability insurance, long-term care insurance—these are the three most effective risk management strategies. I encourage many of my clients to invest in these policies, and I encourage you to do the same. If you're young, you might be thinking, *I don't need all that extra insurance*, in which case I will humbly remind you that you don't need them until you need them, and then you *really* need them.

Remember, to live life is to face risk. So if you can't avoid risk, the goal is to manage and mitigate it the best you can. Put your linebacker, tackler, and cornerback in place so that no single event or tragic mishap can topple your financial health. You may not win every game, but you can still win the championship.

The best defense is a strong offense, which is why you should take action today. Insure your assets against death. Insure your income against disability. Insure your future against unforeseen costs associated with long-term care. Be on the offensive so that you won't be on the *defensive* when tragedy strikes. I hope it never strikes—but if it does, you'll be ready.

Understand Longevity Risk

When I'm speaking to a group of people, I often ask them to name some of the ways in which the world is different today than it was fifty years ago. Inevitably someone will mention the advancement of medicine and the rise of technology. And they are exactly right. These are fantastic developments that have not only improved our quality of life; they have actually extended our life span.

But with every blessing comes attendant challenges. Fifty years ago, if you had a stroke or heart attack, you didn't have to worry about "what came next." You didn't need long-term care, you didn't need a nursing home, and you didn't need a live-in caregiver, because you weren't going to be around. These days, you *are* going to be around. And while that's wonderful for manifold reasons—more time with your spouse, your children, and your grandchildren—it does create some unique issues in the area of financial planning.

In this strategy, we're going to talk about longevity risk—how it affects you, the risk it poses to your finances, and the unique challenges we all face now that we are living longer than ever before.

The Actuarial Table

Every insurance company keeps something called an actuarial table of human mortality—a serious-sounding name for what essentially amounts to a graphical representation of probable life expectancies. Look at any of these tables and you'll see that men are expected to live to be around eighty-five years old, and women to around ninety.

As you might imagine, insurance companies know mortality risk and actuarial science very well; it is, after all, their business. If they didn't have a good sense of how long people were expected to live, their business model would be untenable. They have culled these averages from many decades of study and research, and they're about as accurate as it gets.

So if we use these numbers, and we assume that most people retire, on average, at around sixty-five, you'll see why today's retirees are in a very different position than the retirees of yesteryear. Half a century ago, when a man retired at sixty-five, he typically only lived a few more years. But today, based on the actuarial table, the same man might live another twenty years, while a woman could live twenty-five.

The question that man and woman should be asking themselves is: Do they have enough financial resources to support them through twenty to thirty years of retirement? And that's the right question to ask.

The sad thing is, a lot of people *don't* ask that question and *don't* have enough. They are no longer actively working, so their income dries up several years into retirement, and their savings aren't enough to sustain them for a decade or more. So many men and women are not prepared. Unfortunately, most people spend more time planning for their vacations than for their retirement! The cost of that oversight can be excruciatingly high.

It's Not How Much You Make

Whether you're young or old, the cardinal rule of financial planning is that *we all must live our lives within our means.* Most people live their lives far above their means. Some blow through their retirement money, which expires well before they do. Some live an unsustainable lifestyle, leaving their children to pick up the tab.

Let's say you earn an annual salary of $100,000 working at a tech company. When I first look at your income, I think, "$100,000! Not shabby. That's a pretty decent yearly income for a forty-year-old single woman." But when I get down to brass tacks and delve more deeply into your monthly cash flow, things start to look not so good.

I ask about your budget, and I learn you don't really have one.

That happens more than you think—most people don't have one. They just make what they make and spend what they spend, without any greater awareness about specific dollar amounts. So I work with you and help you ascertain your budget, based on what you are earning and spending every month.

We find you are making $100,000—but you are spending $120,000! If you don't change your spending habits promptly, very soon you will be bankrupt, because unlike the U.S. government, we cannot print money for ourselves.

Remember: It is not how much you make, but how much you *keep* that's important. I cannot say that often enough.

Making—and Keeping—a Budget

If you're at risk of falling into the trap described in the example above, I suggest you make a budget. The simplest way to do it is to write out what we call a cash flow analysis. First, record your income. If you're still working, this will obviously include your salary, but income might also include your pension, social security, and any other money that comes in every month.

Then, record your cash outflow by tracking your expenses every month. Write down what you spend on everything, from mortgage payments to the pack of gum you buy while you're waiting for the mechanic to change your oil (write the oil change down, too).

It's that simple: figure out your income and your expenses. We have software that we use to make it easier for our clients—we basically provide a two-page outline to help them create their budget—but you don't need anything fancy. Figure out your inflow, figure out your outflow, and then figure out how to stanch any excess spending so that you stay within budget.

There are certain "repeat offenders" we see on many clients' budgets. Dining out is one of the big ones. I see many clients spend as much as a quarter of their income dining out. "But I'm always traveling!" you might protest. "Besides, I don't even know how to cook."

I encourage you to buy a beginner's cookbook and learn. First of all, eating out often isn't healthy. And second, the price tag is insane. Sometimes you've got to make painful choices when it comes to cutting things out. Maybe you love going to that fancy restaurant every Friday, or splurging on a new pair of boots every couple of months. I've had clients who spent upwards of $400 getting their hair cut and colored—and they'd do it every six weeks. When you're looking to cut things from your budget, look to the extraneous expenses first. A steak dinner and a snazzy haircut are nice, but they're not worth bankrupting yourself over.

If you're nearing retirement or already there, your budget concerns will naturally change. You will have new needs, and concerns you didn't have before. For example, when I work with my older clients on their budgets, I make sure they always have a cushion. It is crucial that they have money accessible for emergencies, because things can and do happen.

When people move out of the accumulation phase and into the de-accumulation phase, many things shift. The "income" side of your budget sheet will diminish significantly—which may cause an uptick in stress and worry. In fact, some people are so worried, they're postponing their retirement. As I write this book, the unemployment rate in the U.S. is hovering around 7 percent. One of the reasons is that many people who are supposed to retire are not retiring. They are forced to continue working because they don't have enough guaranteed paychecks for life.

Finding the Suitable Strategies

So much of what happens in the world—and to us—is beyond our control, and nowhere is this truer than in the financial markets. Let's say you are withdrawing from your retirement funds at 5 percent. That might be perfectly fine in some markets, but it can be disastrous in others. If your investment is not doing well, you risk potential depletion of the principal. This is one danger people are often not aware of: that if they live for the next thirty years and the market is not in their favor, there is huge potential risk.

When I come to work every day, one of my biggest challenges is making sure that we have good strategies in place for my clients to overcome these risks. We implement a number of different strategies, working to minimize longevity risk. It's all part and parcel of having paychecks for life.[10] For example, when we combine a client's social security and pension with a guaranteed monthly withdrawal from their fixed annuities, it's a potent mix. Not only does the client now have a guaranteed paycheck, they have confidence that they won't run out of money for the rest of their lives.

Here's another thing you have to consider: that you might live *beyond* the average lifespan. Remember the actuarial

10 Guarantees provided are based on the claims paying ability of the issuing company.

tables from the insurance company? Men, on average, live to be eighty-five and women to ninety. But those numbers are exactly that: *averages*. God willing, if you have good genes, eat right, and exercise, you might live to be one hundred!

Alternately, you may die at seventy, or be hit by a bus at sixty-six. And if that happens, you won't need to worry about longevity risk. But of course we hope that doesn't happen, and for most of us, it won't. The fact remains that we do not know when our last day will be. If we did, retirement planning would be easy! (And if you've been lucky enough to inherit a crystal ball, you probably don't need this book.)

I have many clients who are eighty-five and ninety-five years old. They've lived far longer than they expected to, and their lives are fuller than they ever imagined. They are also thanking their lucky stars they were prepared. At this stage of their lives, their primary concern is having enough money to cover day-to-day expenses. And because of the work we've done together, they still have guaranteed paychecks for life.

Do You Have Enough?

No matter where you are in the retirement journey, it's important to ask yourself: Do you have enough?

Do you have enough money to live until your very last day? To cover inflation? To cover long-term care? To cover healthcare? To cover basic day-to-day expenses?

Do you have enough flexibility in your financial plan to provide a cushion so that you are covered in case of emergency or unforeseen events?

In sum: Are you protected against longevity risk, however that risk may manifest itself?

If you answered "No" to most of these questions, or if you don't know the answers, chances are your money is not safe. The sooner you start addressing longevity risk, the more prepared you'll be to live a long, rich life—no matter how long that life turns out to be.

I've said it before and I'll say it again: It is not how much you make, but how much you *keep* that's truly important.

STRATEGY #10

Understand the Sequence-of-Return Risk

The day you retire is more important than you could ever imagine—and it has nothing to do with the party your coworkers throw you or the size of the cake in the break room.

On the day you retire, if the market goes down as opposed to going up, it could have a tremendous impact on how soon you're going to run out of money. A few percentage points can drastically affect the course of your future. There have been studies showing that two men with the same income, the same spending habits, and the same amount of money in their retirement accounts can face drastically different outcomes—*for no other reason than they retired at different points in the market cycle.* A man who retires four years after his twin brother, for example, with all other circumstances being equal, could run out of money *thirteen years sooner* than his twin, simply because the market was heading the opposite way.

This is called the sequence of returns. It's not a very intuitive name, but here's how I describe it to my clients: the sequence is whether the market return is going to go down first, or up first. This is the only sequence we're concerned with. And an unfavorable sequence of returns could force you into a very unpleasant situation. Most people have no idea how devastating this particular risk can be to their retirement futures.

The best way to overcome the sequence-of-return risk is to have income coming in. Let's say, for example, you have a guaranteed[11] income from an annuity, combined with two additional income streams from your pension and social security. Great—you have likely buffered yourself against the mercurial risk of the sequence of returns. It is crucial that you find some way to counteract that risk, because if you don't have that kind of guarantee, you risk running out of money *many years earlier* than you would have otherwise.

Fixed annuities can be a simple and beautiful solution for the sequence-of-return risk, because if you have an annuity, you can take out 4 percent every year. No matter what happens, you are going to get your 4 percent, and

---

11 Guarantees provided are based on the claims paying ability of the issuing company.

whether the market goes up or down, you can depend on that income. You should never run out of money with a plan like this in place.

In these pages, we'll talk more about the sequence-of-return risk and how it can affect you. We will also address the importance of guaranteed income as a way to cushion yourself and your retirement accounts from a volatile sequence of returns. Many well-meaning financial planners often neglect the sequence-of-return risk—and it can absolutely blindside you if you don't find ways to mitigate it. As we said in Strategy #8, the best defense is a strong offense. So let's talk about the ways to defend your retirement by setting up a proactive offense that will keep you and your money safe.

Defining Sequence-of-Return Risk

To illustrate the full range of this risk, I want to consider two different retirees who both retired at sixty-five. They don't know each other. For our purposes we're going to use data that has been proven over a longer period, so let's catapult them both back in time a bit. Imagine these were two separate friends of your parents or grandparents. The first retired in 1969 with $100,000, and the second retired ten years later, in 1979, with the same amount. At the behest of their financial advisors, they both invested in a healthy mix of stocks and bonds. They started their retirement by taking out 5 percent a year, then increased that percentage each year to match inflation.

You might think that they both enjoyed similar retirements, at least on the financial front. At first glance, why wouldn't you think that? But in fact, the ten-year gap between their retirements had a significant impact—which, for one of them, was devastating.

Let's look at some numbers. During the first decade of retirement, the first retiree suffered from negative returns during four of those ten years. In 1969 his ROR was –2.6 percent, in 1973 it was –6.6 percent, in 1974 it was –12.6 percent, and in 1977 it was –2.4 percent. Add that to the fact that inflation rose significantly in the 1970s, and you'll see why he was not a happy camper. By 1979, the year-end value of his portfolio had been depleted to a worrisome $69,487.

But in 1979—the year the second retired, if you'll remember—the market started to recover. That means that for the first ten years of the second retiree's retirement, he didn't experience *any* negative returns. He enjoyed RORs ranging from 3.4 percent on the low end to 23.9 percent on the high end (1980 was a good year). By the end of his first decade of retirement, the year-end value of *his* portfolio was a robust $262,402.

You can probably tell where this is going. The first retiree's retirement funds were totally depleted in fifteen years, thanks to the toxic combination of lower returns and high inflation. The second, on the other hand, experienced smooth sailing well into his nineties. Though he wasn't immune to periods of higher inflation, a positive market performance during those early years and a strong bull market in the 1980s helped his assets continue to grow. In 2008, the year-end value of his portfolio was a staggering $591,402. At ninety-four, he was in an excellent position to leave a legacy for his family, or even to send all three of his grandchildren to college if he so chose.

The most amazing thing about this example is that, if you look at the data, the first retiree actually had a higher average ROR: 10.5 percent, as opposed to the second's 9.6 percent. But averages don't matter nearly as much as the sequence of returns. By eighty, the first was completely out of money—and due to no fault of his own.

This is, perhaps, the most frustrating part of sequence-of-return risk: the fact that it in no way indicates poor or neglectful planning. The first retiree did all the same things the second did—he saved money, he invested it wisely, and he tried to pay attention to what was happening in the market. In the end, it was simply *when* he retired that did him in.

In Life, There Are No Guarantees —Except When There Are

Now let's look at a modern-day example. Let's say you have a typical portfolio. You worked hard at a desk job all through your thirties, forties, and fifties so that you could retire in your sixties and finally see the world with your wife. To help you reach your goal, your financial advisor urges you to keep all your money in certain investments. "These investments are simply the best way to keep your money safe," he says, and because you have always been fairly conservative on the risk spectrum, you believe him.

So you put $100,000 into a CD making 1 percent, and plan to take 5 percent out every year. You're taking out 5 and making 1, meaning you are depleting that mutual fund at 4 percent every year. You will likely run out of money in approximately twenty-five years.

Now, if you only have twenty-five years left, that might work out just fine. You might still have enough money to tour Europe and take an Alaskan cruise with your wife. If you're going to be around for thirty years, however, you're going to run out of money—that's simply a mathematical fact. But both of your parents passed away well before their eightieth birthdays, and you've got enough ongoing health concerns that you in no way expect to outlive your money.

But here's what you have not accounted for (and neither has your advisor): the sequence of returns. If you take out yearly withdrawals of 5 percent from a portfolio that is appreciating each year at a rate *higher* than 5 percent, then bully for you. The withdrawal will have very little effect on your remaining balance. Conversely, if you take 5 percent withdrawals from a portfolio that is *de*preciating, the results could be devastating. Your retirement funds could kick the bucket long before you do.

Now let's look at an alternate reality for you, a world in which your financial advisor takes into account the sequence-of-return risk and directs his clients accordingly. Instead of a mutual fund, your advisor suggests something very different.

"I want to get you into an annuity," the wise advisor says. "It's the only investment that provides tax-deferred treatment of earnings, tax-free transfers, a guaranteed death benefit, and—most important—*guaranteed lifetime income.*"

Your ears perk up immediately. You like the sound of "guaranteed." You grew up with a father who always said, in his gruff way, "In life, son, there are no guarantees." But now, as you are on the cusp of retirement, the one thing you want and need more than anything is a guaranteed income stream for the rest of your life.

You take your advisor's advice and buy an annuity. This particular annuity offers features such as asset allocation and principal protection, which all sounds good to you. You are now able to grow and protect your income in a vehicle that is protected from the maelstrom known as "the sequence of returns." No matter how the market performs, you know your money is safe.

Turns out your father was wrong after all. Sometimes in life, there *are* guarantees. You just have to know where to look.

Make Your Own Luck

Perhaps the best name for sequence-of-return risk would be simply, "bad luck." In no way did the first retiree deserve to have his funds decimated the way they were. He retired at a bad time in the market cycle, and he suffered the consequences. But he didn't do anything to deserve it. He just had very bad luck.

Similarly, the second retiree didn't do anything to deserve his success story. Sure, he was a nice guy who did his best to prepare for the future, but the reason he had over half a million dollars at age ninety-four had nothing to do with his own pluck or foresight. He simply had good luck.

If you're like most of my clients, the thought of basing major retirement decisions on luck is horrifying to you—as well it should be. I'm here to tell you, it doesn't have to be that way. While the sequence of returns will always involve an element of fate and luck, like a ship tossing on uncertain seas, you do not have to be bound to the mast. There are options, strategies, and investment vehicles that will ensure that luck does not work its evil on your money or your happiness.

An annuity is the solution I most often propose to my clients, because I have seen it restore calm and certainty to retirees during even the most tumultuous markets. But there are other solutions, too, which a good planner can help you navigate. The key is to have guaranteed income streams that will not be at the mercy of the market, battered by bear markets or falsely inflated by bulls.

The bottom line is: I don't believe in luck. Or rather, I help my clients make their own luck. When it comes to retiring safely and happily, there really is no other way.

The Three Stars

When a client comes to see me, I like to tell them about the three stars.

"If you want to enjoy life," I say, "if you want to spend time with your children and grandchildren, if you want to have a happy retirement and live out your dreams, remember: the three stars have to be perfectly aligned. If one of them is not aligned, you will be grounded."

At which point they always lean forward, their interest piqued. "What are the three stars?" they ask, as if this were the magic elixir, the answer they've been seeking all their lives.

I smile. "You need to have health, you need to have wealth, and you need to have time."

Those, for me, are the three stars. And every one of those stars has to be shining for you to have a fulfilling retirement.

You wouldn't believe how often I see people who have one or two stars, but not all three. This is, in fact, our default state as human beings. Take some of my older clients, terrific men and women well into their nineties. They've got plenty of money, so they have wealth, and they have all the time in the world—but they are grounded because they don't have health. If they are sick or too weak to travel, they won't be able to hike through Sweden, or go skiing in Aspen, or even visit their grandchildren in Idaho.

If you look at the other end of the spectrum, it's the exact opposite. Most young people have health in spades. They may also have plenty of time, especially if they have no job! And yet, if they aren't working, it probably means they don't have wealth. If they *do* have a job, they've got absolutely no time, because they spend it all working. So young people are grounded, too, missing at least one of the three stars.

There is a perfect window in the lives of most of my clients, when all three stars are within reach. For those of us who are blessed, it could be five or ten or even twenty years. For others, it might be no time at all. Let's say a friend retires early at fifty-five, eager to embark on his many plans and the exciting years that lie ahead. On the very day he retires, there is a light rain, and the wind knocks one of his neighbor's tree branches into his yard. He goes out back and is trying to clean up the branches when a bolt of lightning strikes the tree, killing him instantly. It was a tragedy no one saw coming.

I tell this story as a sobering reminder that we never know what's coming down the pike. This is why I encourage all my clients to make use of the time they have and to enjoy the more intangible things life has to offer. A client who retires at fifty-five might have plenty of wealth, and time is just opening up to him—but then again, his health might take a sudden and horrific turn.

There is a limited window of opportunity in our lives when those three stars are in perfect alignment. While the story above is an extreme example, it's a kind of wake-up call, a reminder that none of us can see the future. All we can do is use the time, health, and wealth we *do* have the best we can.

When the Stars Align

The work I do every day, the work that makes me eager to get out of bed every morning, is the work of helping my clients get their three stars aligned. It's all about establishing health, wealth, and time.

Now, I'm not a medical doctor, so my strategies will never be directly about your health. I won't tell you to take this supplement or that pill, or to exercise five times a week and eat lots of leafy vegetables. But I *can* help you keep your financial house in order, which reduces stress—and if you've got less stress, you will probably be healthier. When it comes to the first star, that's really all I can do.

When it comes to wealth and time—the second and third stars—the work I do has a far more direct impact. If you take care of your finances and save enough and understand how your money is invested and why, then you'll never have to go back to work out of desperation. Most likely, you will be able to retire at sixty-five, and—barring unforeseen accidents or illnesses—you will have all the time in the world to do all the things you want to do. So, indirectly, I've created time for you. Because if you're still working into your sixties and seventies because you haven't saved enough, then you won't be able to enjoy that third star of time.

Everyone's stars shine a little differently, meaning that health, wealth, and time will manifest in your life in unique ways. This is why I consider it paramount to know my clients, to *really* know them. FINRA, the largest independent securities regulator in the U.S., recently passed a rule called KYC: know your client. But this has been a cornerstone of my business long before FINRA put it down in ink. Knowing my clients is absolutely fundamental to helping them create the retirement they want.

In my first meeting with a client, I am trying to learn as much about his or her background as I can. We have what we call a financial planning guide, a four-page document we ask all new clients to fill out. They have to do a little homework to list out their goals, their objectives, and what they're trying to accomplish. We are also interested in what they have accumulated so far, and any problems or challenges they are trying to address. If I do not know their history and where they are today, I won't be able to solve their problems by providing tailored solutions based on the many strategies in my toolkit.

Our initial goal is to devise a game plan. The game plan is the macro perspective, the "big picture" of how we will work together. I believe you always need the view of the forest before you zero in on the view of the trees.

After we've got a game plan, we move on from there. I focus on a client's most immediate needs first. Some needs can wait, while others are urgent. And sometimes, if clients or their financial planners have made mistakes in the past, they can have serious repercussions if we don't fix them as soon as possible.

Often new clients are in such precarious positions when they come to see me that it takes more than one meeting to implement the changes I want to make. I'm not talking about incidental tweaks and adjustments; it's more like a transformational sea change. Usually we have at least three meetings, and often we need to make adjustments every six months, or once a year. As with most things done right, this takes time, making it all the more important that you work with someone who understands your unique situation and what you want to accomplish.

I won't lie to you: it can be overwhelming at the beginning. This is why you want an advisor who will not become mired in "paralysis by analysis," as the saying goes. I have known planners who, daunted by the number of "fixes" they need to make for their new clients, do nothing instead. That's not good. You want someone who will work proactively to get you and your money into a safer place as soon as possible. As we discussed in Strategy #10, when it comes to retirement, the difference of a few months or years can have huge repercussions.

As I write this book, I am moving into the twenty-second year of my practice. I've seen and experienced a lot of things doing this work, and I've learned from all of them. I've learned that knowing theory is one thing, but having real-life experience helping people brings substantial value to the table. That's one of the assets I can offer my clients: more than two decades of experience "in the trenches."

A second advantage I offer my clients is the value of being an independent financial advisor. Because I don't work for a specific company, I do not have a specific agenda, meaning I can be much more objective when giving advice. I'm not pushing or discussing one particular strategy or product.

I can truly tailor my financial advice to *you*—which has been a huge benefit for everyone I've ever worked with.

Then there's benefit number three: I am a Chartered Life Underwriter, a Chartered Financial Consultant, and a Certified Estate Planner. These designations mean I have years of study under my belt, and a large pool of knowledge from which to draw. And you're not just dealing with me. As we discussed in Strategy #7, we have a whole team of experts—estate-planning attorneys, eldercare attorneys, CPAs, you name it—and we work as a team. That means you will have access to counselors and advisers in many different areas of expertise, people who can help you in myriad ways. As I said earlier, I like to think of my job as being the quarterback, coordinating the efforts of a championship team.

One of my greatest points of pride in the work I do is that my clients trust me with some of the most important decisions of their lives. My name is written on their most important papers, the documents that determine the course of not just their future, but also the futures of their children and grandchildren. I had a client, a lovely woman, who passed away three years ago at sixty-two years young. We were all very upset by her sudden passing—she died after a hospital procedure went wrong.

After she was gone, her grown children called me up. Apparently this woman had written a letter and put it with all her most important documents, telling her children,

"When I am no longer around, please make sure you see Stephen Ng."

They showed me the note, and I can't possibly express the pride I felt in seeing it. To know that I was an important person in this woman's life, so important that I was the one she wanted her children to turn to if something were to happen. I think that is the greatest compliment, to know that what I do and what I give have incredible consequences for the legacy my clients are going to pass on to the next generation. That, to me, is a great honor. These clients have entrusted me with so much, and I do not take that responsibility lightly.

An Invitation

I love sharing from my knowledge base to help others prepare for the future. If I can help just one person have a happy and secure retirement, I've done my job. In every interview I've given—whether it was for the *Wall Street Journal*, Fox, Christian Television Network, or the many others I've done—my goal has been to educate and inform, to motivate others to start thinking about their retirement and making the right choices. I'd love to do the same for you.

If what you have read in these pages has resonated with you, I encourage you to reach out to me by phone at (973) 218-9600, or e-mail me at SNg@StephenNgFG.com so we can continue the conversation.

I hope this book has been a compelling call to action, a catalyst for seizing the many financial opportunities available to you. I hope you have seen yourself in the retirees described here, and gotten excited by the advice and strategies I have provided. Your future is your decision. Whether or not our paths cross, I wish you all the best on your own journey. May all three stars shine brightly upon you, blessing your golden years with health, wealth, and time, ensuring that your future is positively luminous.

CPSIA information can be obtained
at www.ICGtesting.com
Printed in the USA
FFOW05n1026280217